Vivaldi

Cover design and art direction by Pearce Marchbank Studio
Cover photography by Julian Hawkins

Printed and bound in Hungary

Hardback
Order No. OP44593
ISBN 0.7119.1406.0

Softback
Order No. OP45202
ISBN 0.7119.1727.2

Exclusive Distributors:
Book Sales Limited,
8/9 Frith Street,
London W1V 5TZ,
England.
Music Sales Pty Limited,
120 Rothschild Avenue,
Rosebery,
Sydney,
NSW 2018,
Australia.
To The Music Trade Only:
Music Sales Limited,
8/9 Frith Street,
London W1V 5TZ,
England.
Music Sales Corporation,
24 East 22nd Street,
New York,
NY10010,
U.S.A.

The Illustrated Lives of the Great Composers.

Vivaldi

John Booth

Omnibus Press
London/New York/Sydney/Cologne

Other titles in the series

Contents

Acknowledgements

Grateful thanks are due to a number of people who have been most generous with their assistance. They are too numerous to name but mention should be made of Dorothy Daly of Padua for local research, to Guy Booth for picture research and to Vivienne Couldrey for help in translation.

Photographs by John Booth.

Bibliography

Brinton, S. *Venice Past and Present* (London 1925)

Burney, C. *A General History of Music* (London 1776-89) 4 vols.

Cande de R. *Vivaldi* (Paris, 1967)

Cande de R. (with others) *Vivaldi* (Paris 1975)

Evelyn, J. *Diary* (London 1818)

Kendall, A. *Vivaldi, His Music, Life and Times* (London 1978)

Kolneder, W. *Vivaldi, His Life and Work* (Germany 1965, London 1970)

Levey, M. *The Venetian Scene* (London 1973)

Monet, J. *Casanova's Memoirs* (New York 1946)

Morris, J. *Venice* (London 1960)

Morris, J. *The Venetian Empire, A Sea Voyage* (London 1980)

Moore, R. I. (general editor) *The Hamlyn Historical Atlas*

O'Brien, G. *The Golden Age of Italian Music* (London 1947)

Pincherle, M. *Antonio Vivaldi et la musique instrumentale* (Paris 1948)

Pincherle, M. *Vivaldi* (Paris 1955). Published in English 1958 as *Vivaldi, Genius of the Baroque*, translated by Christopher Hatch.

Ruskin, J. *The Stones of Venice* (London 1851-3)

Talbot, M. *Vivaldi* (London 1978)

Voltaire *Candide* (Paris 1759)

A Poeta di Musica de la Sua...
d. Musica de Sua...
L. opera a Granmentea 1723.

Chapter 1

Origins

Vivaldi is one of those rare composers whose work cuts across the usual divisions of classical and 'other' music. His music has a freshness and vitality which reaches 20th-century listeners as effortlessly as it did those of the 18th century when the music was first heard. Perhaps this appeal can be explained by the sense of a powerful human presence in his work, an irrepressible, energetic personality. Yet, while his music is accessible, he is distant. Behind the easily approachable music the composer is shadowy and elusive. Information about his life is surprisingly sparse; there are many gaps and mysteries in his story. What we do know about his life is fascinating, what we do not know adds to this fascination.

He was born in 1678 in Venice, in the district of Castello in the parish of San Martino. The precise date of his birth was established only in the early 1960s and many books still give his date of birth as 1675. The discovery of the record of his baptism in the small church of San Giovanni in Bragora established the facts beyond doubt. The parish records show that on 6 May 1678 'Antonio Lucio, son of Signor Giovanni Battista Vivaldi, son of the late Camillo, born on 4th March last, who was baptised at home, being in danger of death, by the midwife, Madam Margarete Veronese. Today he was brought to the church where he received the exorcisms and holy oils from me, Giacomo Foranciero, parish priest. His godfather was Antonio Veccelio, son of the late Gerolemo, apothecary, at the sign of the dose in the parish.'

So Vivaldi was a weak child at birth; his health was to be a recurring problem throughout his life. His background was humble, although not poor. His father, Giovanni Battista, born in Brescia in 1655, was a barber by trade but he was also a violinist of ability.

Giovanni married Camilla Calicchio, a tailor's daughter, on 6 August 1677, and Antonio came into the world, as we have seen, quite promptly after their union – perhaps prematurely or

The only true likeness of Vivaldi we know. It was the work of Pier Leono Ghezzi (1674-1755) and was drawn when Vivaldi was in Rome in 1723. The inscription reads: "The red priest, the composer who did the opera at the Capranica in 1723."

Vivaldi's baptism certificate.

conceived out of wedlock. In any event, Antonio was not baptised in Church until two months after his birth, probably because of ill health.

His father's family came from Brescia, famous for violin makers. Giovanni and his family left Brescia for Venice where Giovanni continued his work as barber and musician but it was not long before he was working only as a violinist. Evidently he possessed exceptional musical ability as he became a violinist at the ducal chapel of San Marco in 1685 which was the principal music establishment of the city. In 1713 he was listed in a guidebook for visitors to Venice, *Guida dei Foresterieri*, as one of the best violinists in Venice under the title of virtuoso, along with his son, Antonio, who had become famous by that time.

Antonio inherited his father's ability as a violinist and he also inherited another characteristic: red hair. Giovanni is referred to in the registers of San Marco as Rossi and Antonio came to be known as the 'red-haired priest' (*il prete rosso*).

Antonio Vivaldi was the eldest of the six children of the marriage. The others were Margarita Gabriela, Cecilia Maria, Benaventure Tomaso, Zanetta Ann and Francesco. None of the others became musicians and Francesco followed his father's original calling of barber and wigmaker. He seems to have been a young man of high spirits and independence as he was banished from Venice for a time for using insulting behaviour towards a nobleman.

There may have been another brother, Giuseppe Vivaldi, who was as hotblooded as Francesco for he was sentenced to be banished from Venice for five years for wounding a grocer boy in an incident near the church of San Giovanni Crisostomo. This took place in 1729, when Antonio Vivaldi was already a well-known figure in the city, as can be seen in the statement by a witness at the trial

A plaque on the walls of San Giovanni di Bragora announces that *Il Prete Rosso*, born on 4 March, 1678, was baptised there.

who said he did not know Giuseppe's surname but recognised him as 'a brother of the red-haired priest who plays the violin' *(fratello del prete rosso che sona il violin)*. Musicologists now doubt that Giuseppe was a member of Antonio Vivaldi's family but the incident informs us about his standing and the spirit of the times.

Little is known about Vivaldi's childhood except that the family lived in the district of Castello – one of six districts into which Venice was, and still is, divided. Today, it is much as it was then, a labyrinth of narrow alleys and canals and bridges between the Riva degli Schiavoni to the Arsenal, the naval dockyard which played a vital part in the history of Venice. Vivaldi lived most of his life in this densely populated area near the heart of the city, the Piazza of San Marco and the commercial centre, the Rialto.

It is assumed that the young Vivaldi received his early musical training from his father and from the musicians of San Marco, possibly from Giovanni Legrenzi (1626-1690) who was choirmaster at San Marco at the time. A composer of operas and much instrumental and sacred music, Legrenzi is known to have had Gasparini and Lotti as pupils and, possibly, Albinoni. As he died when Vivaldi was only twelve, some experts believe it is unlikely there was a master-pupil relationship but it seems possible. Certainly Vivaldi would be familiar with the music of San Marco and it is said that when very young he deputised for his father.

It is impossible to examine Vivaldi without examining Venice. He was a child of his city and the special time in which he lived. His music might be a metaphor for the city state that was Venice, which was a wonder of the world then as it had been for centuries. The Most Serene Republic, Serenissima, a gilded, glittering marvel

The narrow streets and canals around the church of San Martino where Vivaldi lived for most of his life in Venice.

The entrance to the Arsenal, the source of Venice's maritime power, the greatest dockyard in the world during the Serenissima's centuries of power. 16,000 worked here during the 16th century, providing the galleys that sustained the Republic's power.

The Arsenal is only a short distance from the parish church of San Martino with which Vivaldi and his father were associated.

rising out of the grey Adriatic sea, a monument to man's power over nature, a triumph of imagination. The world flocked to it; princes and ambassadors, men of letters and of fashion, traffic which continues to this day with the crowds milling in the modern Piazza of San Marco, posing for the cameras, feeding pigeons which are so fat they can scarcely fly.

But Venice was much more than a fabled visual wonder. The

Venetian Republic had a large and powerful empire. It was a great maritime power with colonial possessions – Crete, Cyprus and Constantinople. The Arsenal was the biggest shipyard in the world; in the 16th century more than 15,000 people worked there: at one time a new ship was launched every day. The Venetian navy ruled the waves on behalf of a state which was independent of east and west, dedicated to the interests of Venice, trading with all, enjoying the advantages of its geographical position on the vital trade routes between east and west.

The city itself had been born when people fled from the mainland of the Veneto, and the attentions of the barbarians, to the misty reaches of the lagoon. It was there that the city state evolved, the founding date is given as 25 March 421, becoming a republic based on the Roman pattern with a doge as an elected non-hereditary ruler: doge is a Venetian corruption of the Italian word *duce*, or leader.

Trade strengthened the republic's position, especially after the Fourth Crusade at the beginning of the 13th century which gained Venice a string of colonial possessions throughout the Aegean. When Vivaldi was born at the end of the 17th century, Venice still had the appearance and trappings of a great power but that power was waning. The first loosening of the reins of trade power came with the triumphant voyage of Vasco da Gama in 1499 rounding the Cape to India, opening up a new trade route and breaking the Venetian monopoly of the trade route between east and west.

That which had been taken by conquest was to be relinquished

During the last three centuries of the Republic, Venice's greatest rivals were the Turks who gradually pushed Venetian maritime power back to the Adriatic. The Turkish domain even stretched to parts of the Austro-Hungarian Empire. This contemporary engraving depicts the Great Siege of Vienna by the Turks in 1683 when the capital was relieved by the Imperial Army. The conflicts between the Venetians and Turks were reflected in Vivaldi's music, especially in the sacred military oratorio Juditha Triumphans in 1716.

in the same manner. The principal threat was the rise of the Muslim empire. Constantinople had been taken by the ancient blind Doge Dandolo at the time of the Fourth Crusade, a victory that established Venetian power and enriched her in many ways – not least in the treasures taken from ancient Byzantium, including the four magnificent horses which were to become a symbol of Venice

The pageantry of Venice captured in this painting of a procession to San Marco by Gentile Bellini (1429-1507).

from their stalls on the façade of San Marco. The prize was re-taken by the Turks in 1453 and although Venice continued to be a dominant influence in the region, the last three centuries of the Republic were a gradual decline.

When Vivaldi was young, the Republic had another century of life before it. The glittering city was still a wonder of the world. As its real might faded, it became self-absorbed, indulgent, carnal, devoted to the gratification of the senses, the pursuit of pleasure. It had always been in love with spectacle, parades, processions, richly decorated buildings, sumptuous clothes, regattas, and the paintings of Gentile Bellini and Vittore Carpaccio give some evidence of the splendour of public life.

Since the 12th century every doge had celebrated Venice's connection with the surrounding water with a mystical marriage to the sea. On Ascension Day the doge and his ministers of state in the magnificent ducal galley, Bucenataur, attended by ambassadors and other nobles, led a stately procession to sea where the doge threw a consecrated ring into the waves with the words:

15

Desponamus te, Mare, in signum veri perpetique dominii (We wed thee, O sea, in sign of veritable and perpetual domination).

In the 18th century the parade of distinguished visitors continued, providing reasons for further lavish spectacle. Frederick IV of Denmark and Norway, the Prince of Poland and Saxony, the Elector of Bavaria, the Crown Prince of Modena, the Queen of the Kingdom of the Two Sicilies, all were greeted with programmes for their entertainment. A central part of these entertainments was the music, for Venice was a city which resounded to music. The people had a mania for it at all levels of society. Aristocrats composed and played, just as gondoliers serenaded through the night. John Evelyn described a visit in 1645 when the canal was like 'Hyde Park', where ladies and gentlemen were 'singing, playing on harpsichords, and other music, and serenading their mistresses'. Charles de Brosse, French traveller and first president of the parliament of Dijon, wondered in 1739 at the Venetian passion for music: 'The infatuation of the nation for this art is inconceivable'.

Doctor Charles Burney noted in 1745:

The canals are crowded with musical people at night, bands of music, French horns, duet singers in every gondola.

Music was heard always, everywhere, by gondoliers, bakers and other tradesmen, a random, spontaneous outpouring. Again Doctor Burney noted in 1745 when he arrived at his inn:

A band of musicians consisting of two good fiddles, a violin cello and female voice stopped under the windows and performed in such a manner as would have made people stare in England but here they were as little attended to as coalmen or oyster women are with us.

Visitors were struck not only by the Venetians' passionate attachment to music but the ability they showed in it. P. J. Grosley in 1764 reported:

A shoemaker or a smith dressed in his work clothes, starts a tune; other people of his sort join in with him and sing this tune in parts with accuracy, precision and taste that is scarcely to be met with in fashionable society in our northern lands.

The main centres of the music were, of course, the churches. Venice was then a city of churches, as it is today, from the splendour of San Marco to the dozens of smaller churches dotted throughout the city, yet even here it was said that women would weep, cry out and faint away when hearing the solemn chants of the church or the voice of some famous singer.

Dr Charles Burney (1726-1814), a portrait by Reynolds. Dr Burney was a minor composer and musicologist, author of a four-volume History of Music and of works dealing with his travels, including accounts of his experiences in Venice. He knew Vivaldi's music well and is an invaluable source of information on the musical life of Venice in the 18th century.

Venice was a city echoing with music, part of the very air of the place; its people were swept along by it, soothed by it, aroused and elated by it. It is easy to imagine what such an atmosphere would have been to any young man, but especially to a young man like Vivaldi who was born to music. His family was of modest origins and it was not uncommon for the bright sons of such families to enter the Church. His father's work as a violinist at San Marco would have meant regular contacts with the priesthood and it was, perhaps, here that he received encouragement to enter the Church.

There is no evidence that he attended any college of religious education. It seems likely that he was attached to a church as an assistant and studied during this period. Documents in the Archivo Patriarcale in Venice suggest he was attached to the churches of S. Geminiani and S. Giovanni in Oleo.

He was tonsured at the age of fifteen-and-a-half on 18 September, 1693 and his ecclesiastical progress was as follows:

Minor Orders
Porter (Ostario) 19 September 1693
Lector (Lettore) 21 September 1694
Exorcist (Esorcista) 25 December 1695
Scolyte (Accolite) 21 September 1696
Holy Orders
Sub deacon (Suddiacone) 4 April 1699
Deacon (Iadcone) 18 September 1700
Priest (Sacerdote) 23 March 1703

This progress to priesthood took almost ten years, an unusually long time, which may be explained by Vivaldi's poor health; a constant theme in his life. It has been suggested that Vivaldi used the church simply as a means of furthering his musical career and evidence for this charge was cited by the fact that he never officiated as a priest after receiving Holy Orders. Religion was a convenience, the knowing said, and music was his true vocation.

Further evidence is cited in a story circulated in his own time and recounted, no doubt with embellishment and certainly with enthusiasm, by successive writers such as P. L. Roualle de Boisgelou in his *Table Biographique* and Count Grégoire Orloff's *Essai sur l'histoire de la musique en Italie*. De Boisgelou's account, written about 1800, is graphic:

One day when Vivaldi was saying Mass, a fugue subject came into his mind. He at once left the altar where he was officiating and repaired to the sacristy to write out his theme, then he came back to finish the Mass.

It is a good story and one that would be much enjoyed in the telling. The author adds:

He was reported to the Inquisition, which happily looked on him as a musician, that is, as a madman, and limited itself to forbidding him to say Mass from that time forward.

Happily – and unusually – we have Vivaldi's own explanation of how this story came into circulation. In a letter to one of his patrons, Marchese Guido Bentivoglio, of 16 November 1737, Vivaldi writes:

It was twenty-five years ago that I said Mass for what will be the last time, not to interdiction or at anyone's behest, as His Eminence can appraise himself, but my own decision on account of an ailment that has burdened me since birth. When I had barely been ordained a priest I said Mass for a year or a little more. Then I discontinued saying it, having on three occasions had to leave the altar without completing it because of this ailment. For this same reason I nearly always live at home, and I only go out in a gondola or coach because I can no longer walk on account of this chest ailment or, rather, tightness in the chest.

Vivaldi was almost sixty when this letter was written and it is likely his health had deteriorated. His description does not fit the man of the compositions and travels: furiously energetic in both. He goes on to say that he never said Mass in Rome during the three opera seasons – reminding his patron that he played for the Pope – or in Mantua or Vienna. And he concludes:

My travels have always been very costly because I have always had to make them with four or five persons to assist me.

His illness has been diagnosed as asthma or angina pectoris, a condition which was to have a crucial influence on his life.

Chapter 2

Pietà

Shortly after being ordained, perhaps soon after deciding it was no longer possible to say Mass and therefore to continue the religious life of a priest, Vivaldi's name appears in the records of an establishment which was to be a part of his life, with interruptions, for the next forty years, the Pietà. The records of the Seminario musicale dell'Ospidale della Pietà for 1703 show that Don Antonio Vivaldi, Maestro di Violino, received thirty ducats for duties as a teacher of the violin.

The Pietà was a remarkable institution, one of a number in Venice. It was an orphanage for girls which provided its charges with a home and musical education and was one of four such institutions in Venice – the others were the Incurabili, the Mendicanti, the Santa Giovanni e Paolo. There is a large body of testimony about these establishments which were a subject of great interest to foreign visitors, to judge from the number of accounts which were written about them. These charitable institutions – called Ospedali because they were originally attached to a hospital – were established to care for children, many of them illegitimate. They had been set up in the 14th century to cope with the problem of a growing number of homeless children; at one time it was estimated that the Ospedali were caring for more than 6,000 of them.

In the early years of the 17th century, an indefatigable English traveller, Thomas Coryate, wrote bluntly of the purpose of the Pietà at that time:

If any of them (courtesans) happen to have any children (as indeed they have but few, for according to the old proverbs the best carpenters make the fewest chips), they are brought up at their own charge or in a certain house in the cities appointed for no other use but only for the bringing up of the courtesan bastards, which I saw eastward above Saint Markes near to the sea side. In the south wall of which building that looketh towards the sea, I observed a certain yron grate inserted into a hollow

The church of La Pietà, enlarged and reconstructed in 1745, was the chapel for the Ospedale della Pietà, the orphanage for girls with which Vivaldi was associated for most of his life as a teacher and composer. The Pietà was one of four Ospedali in Venice which were originally founded to care for orphaned and illegitimate children in the city but later developed into establishments which provided a general and musical education for the girls. The musical standards at the Ospedali were extraordinarily high and widely admired by visitors to the city and there was considerable rivalry between them.

peece of the wall, betwixt which grate and a plaine stone beneath it, there is a convenient little space to put an infant.

The original church was reconstructed in 1745 but it stands on the same spot 'eastward above Saint Markes near to the sea side'. It is on the Riva degli Schiavoni, a short stroll from the Doge's Palace, near the Ponte del Sepolcro, and faces the beautiful outline of the island of S. Giorgo Maggiore.

Thomas Coryate was a learned traveller whose account of a European journey he made in 1608 was published as *Coryate's Crudities*. It was widely read and has the distinction of being satirised by John Donne (1572-1631) who wrote:

Venice vast lake thou hadst seen, and would seek then some vaster thing, and foundst a courtesan.

The reference to the courtesan is an allusion to the famous courtesans of the city which the traveller admired greatly.

Another Englishman, Edward Wright, in his book *Some Observations Made in Travelling through France, Italy . . .* in 1720-22 observes:

Those put into the Pietà are generally bastards. There is a prodigious number of children taken care of in this hospital; they say they amount to at least six thousand, and that before the erection of this charity multitudes used to be found which had been thrown into canals of the city.

Given the number of children cared for, it is unlikely they were all illegitimate, although there were almost 12,000 courtesans in Venice at the end of the 16th century according to official figures. Many would have been orphaned, perhaps losing parents in one of the Republic's many overseas military adventures. Credit for the founding of the orphanage of the Pietà is given to Brother Pieruzzo in 1346 who founded the first at the church of San Francesco della Vigna (the name commemorates the gift of a vineyard to the Franciscans in 1253), and a later one at San Giovanni in Bragora where Vivaldi was baptised.

San Giovanni di Bragora, in a serene campo in Venice, where Vivaldi was baptised on 6 May, 1678. This information was not discovered until the 1960s when the documents were found in the parish registers. Brother Pieruzzo, who is credited with the foundation of the first establishment for the care of abandoned and illegitimate children of Venice at San Francesco della Vigna, added another establishment in the parish of San Giovanni di Bragora in 1348 which was to become the Pietà.

The famous Ospedale has gone, but in a narrow alley which runs past the Pietà an ancient notice can be seen to this day which carries a warning to the passer-by:

May the Lord God strike with curses and excommunications those who send, or permit their sons and daughters – whether legitimate or natural – to be sent to this Hospital of the Pietà, having the means and ability to bring them up, for they will be obliged to pay back every expense and amount spent on them, neither may they be absolved unless they make atonement as is clearly set out in the bull of our Lord Pope Paul dated ADL 12 1548.

A fierce warning in stone on the wall of the church of La Pietà which would have been a commonplace sight to Vivaldi on his journeys from the Ospedali to the chapel.

By the time Vivaldi took up his duties at the Pietà, the Ospedali were famous. They had developed from institutions simply providing shelter and now provided education of a general and musical kind. More significantly they were for girls only although the inscription above suggests both boys and girls were accepted earlier. The Ospedali were supported by the state and run by a board of governors which was appointed by the Senate.

At the Pietà in Vivaldi's time there were about 1,000 girls, a considerable establishment. The élite of the girls were those who received a specifically musical education, the *figli di coro*, while the others – a majority – were the *figli di commun* who received a general education.

Maintaining the Pietà, as well as the other Ospedali, was expensive, even with the help of the state and private donations.

One of the ways money was raised was from concerts organised by the Ospedali and there was great musical rivalry between the four establishments.

Not surprisingly, the *figli di coro* were the stars and the board of governors gave much thought to maintaining musical standards and improving them. In the early 18th century the musical ability of the girls of the Ospedali was one of the wonders of Venice and they had become an attraction for visiting tourists, many of whom have left detailed accounts of them.

In 1698 the Russian Petre Andreevic Tolstago wrote:

In Venice there are convents where the women play the organ and other instruments, and sing so wonderfully that nowhere else in the world could one find such sweet and harmonious song. Therefore people come to Venice from all parts with the wish to refresh themselves with these angelic songs, above all those of the Convent of the Incurables.

Edward Wright favoured the music of the Pietà:

Every Sunday and holiday there is a performance of music in the chapels of these hospitals, vocal and instrumental, performed by the young women of the places who are set in a gallery above and, though not professed, are hid from any distinct view of those below by a lattice of ironwork. The organ parts, as well as those of other instruments, are all performed by the young women. They have a eunuch for their master and he composes their music. Their performance is surprisingly good, and many excellent voices are among them. And this is all the more amusing since their persons are concealed from view.

The reference to the composer of the music being a eunuch is a little surprising if it refers, as seems likely, to Vivaldi. It is possible the Englishman was told, or assumed, that only a eunuch would be permitted to be in close contact with so many young women. There is no other evidence to support the assertion; indeed, if it were true certain allegations about Vivaldi's association with a singer, Anna Girò – which we shall deal with later on – would never have been made or, at least, quickly dismissed.

Alan Kendall, in his book on Vivaldi published in 1978, produces a curious piece of information, a letter from François Mission dated 14 February 1688, which deals with priests following a musical career:

They have found a means to accommodate the affair, and have concluded that a priest fitted for musick may exercise the priesthood as well as another; provided he hath his necessities or, if you will, his superfluities in his pocket.

Kendall explains that necessities is a reference to testicles, as is superfluities since they were theoretically superfluous because the clergy were supposed to be celibate. It may be that having them 'in his pocket' is a reference to having them removed: which supports the idea that priests in posts similar to that of Vivaldi might well have been eunuchs.

Charles de Brosses (1709-77, historian and parliamentarian) was enraptured by the music of the Ospedali:

The transcendent music is that of the asylums. There are four of them, made up of illegitimate and orphaned girls and whose parents are not in a position to raise them. They are brought up at the expense of the state and trained solely to excel in music. Moreover, they sing like angels and play the violin, flute, the organ, the oboe, the cello and the bassoon; in short, there is no instrument, however unwieldy, that can frighten them. They are cloistered like nuns. It is they alone who perform, and about forty girls take part in each concert. I vow to you that there is nothing so diverting as the sight of a young and pretty nun in white habit, with a bunch of pomegranate blossoms over her ear, conducting the orchestra and beating time with all the grace and precision imaginable.

De Brosses seems to have enjoyed an uninterrupted view of the musicians, which would not have been possible at the Pietà and other establishments, as described by Edward Wright and supported by Jean-Jacques Rousseau in his Confessions, dating from around 1743, although he was writing about the Mendicanti:

Music of a kind that is very superior in my opinion to that of the operas and that has not its equal through Italy or perhaps the world is that of the scuole. Every Sunday at the church of these four scuole during vespers, motets for a large chorus with a large orchestra, which are composed and directed by the greatest masters in Italy, are performed in barred-off galleries solely by girls, of whom the oldest is not twenty years of age. I can conceive of nothing as voluptuous, as moving, as this music. The church is always full of music lovers, even the singers from the Venetian opera come so as to develop genuine taste in singing based on these excellent models. What grieved me was those accursed grilles which allowed only tones to go through and concealed the angels of loveliness of whom they were worthy.

There are a number of paintings which illustrate musical performances by the young women of the Ospedali and one of the best known by Guardi (in the Munich Pinakothek) shows a concert in a convent without a grille. Von Poellnitz, writing in about 1729, gives a revealing glimpse of a typical concert:

I am in some doubt whether I should reckon the music of the Venetian churches in the number of its pleasures; but, on the whole, I think I ought, because certainly their churches are frequented more to please

24

The reception room or parlour of a convent pictured here in this painting by Francesco Guardi (1712-93), a contemporary of Vivaldi. The painting is one of a number from the period which confirm that life in the convents of Venice was not particularly austere. Some observers felt the sisters were more interested in theatre and fashion than religion and prayer.

the ear than for real devotion. The church of La Pietà which belongs to the nuns who know no other father but love, is more frequented. These nuns are entered very young, and are taught music, and to play on all sorts of instruments, in which some of them are excellent performers. Apollonia actually passes for the finest singer and Anna-Maria's for the first violin in Italy. The concourse of people to this church on Sundays and holidays is quite extraordinary. 'Tis the rendezvous of all the coquettes of Venice, and such as are fond of intrigues have here both their hands and hearts full. Not many days after my arrival in this city I was at this very church, where was a vast audience, and the finest music.

Charles de Brosses, a fervent admirer of the ladies of the Ospedali, confirms their reputation for musicianship:

Zabetta, of the Incurabili, who is above all astonishing for the range of her voice and the attacks that she has in her throat as if she were playing Somis' violin. She carries off all the votes; one would be offering oneself to be beaten by the populace in equalling anyone to her, but whilst no

Domenico Scarlatti (1685-1757), composer and harpsichordist, who was a pupil of Gasparini, maestro di coro at the Pietà, and who met Handel in Venice and may have met Vivaldi, although there is no record of the event.

one is listening, I will whisper in your ear that Margarita of the Mendicanti is well worth it and pleases me better. The one of the four Ospedali I visit most often, and where I enjoy myself most, is the Ospedale della Pietà; it is also the first for the perfection of the symphonies. What strictness of execution! It is only there that one hears the first attack of the bow, so falsely vaunted at the Paris Opéra.

Vivaldi was in good musical company at the Pietà. Leading musicians such as Domenico Scarlatti, Legrenzi, Caldara, Galuppi, Hasse and others worked closely with the leading Ospedali.

The theatrical nature of many of these musical occasions is shown by the fact that the libretto of the oratorio to be performed would be handed out at the door of the church and the names of the solo singers given prominence. Behaviour had not become so lax that applause was permitted in the churches and the manner of showing approval was by coughing, shuffling of feet and similar noises.

When Vivaldi took up his duties at the Pietà, the *maestro di coro* was Francesco Gasparini (1668-1727). Vivaldi's first duties were as a violin teacher although his duties were soon increased. In August 1704 the records of the deliberations of the governors of the Pietà show that 'since the sustained efforts of Don Antonio Vivaldi, the girls' violin teacher, have borne fruit and since he has also rendered diligent assistance in the tuition of the viola inglese' the sum of 40 ducats was added to his salary, making a total of 100 ducats per annum.

The governors of the Pietà were scrupulous in their concern for every facet of the establishment. The girls with musical ability, the *figli di coro*, were given special consideration. They might be sent to the country for their health, as was the case with Apollonia when a Doctor Bozzato affirmed on 6 June 1741 that 'on account of her indispositions she should be sent to the open air' as should Alina 'because of all her indispositions'. They were the aristocrats of the establishment, and an integral part of the life of the Pietà. The older girls taught the younger girls; the most senior being given the title of *Maestra* to which was added the instrument they played – Maestra Lucietta della Viola, Maestra Silvia dal Violino, Maestra Luciana Organista. They had real authority, not only over the other girls but over their teachers, since they signed the quarterly accounts which certified that individual teachers had performed their duties efficiently. They were also paid for their work: 80 ducats a year.

An example of the way the Pietà was run is the report of the governors for December 1744, when the petition of Maestra Michieletta del Violin for an additional basket of wood for each week for eight months was considered. The request was dealt with most judicially; it is remembered that in December 1729, Michieletta was given two baskets of wood a week for the four

26

winter months and had been given an additional basket of wood each week for the rest of the year in 1735. The evidence was pored over thoroughly and Michieletta received the additional basket of wood she had requested.

The musicians of the Pietà were much admired, and not only for their music. Many received proposals of marriage. The German flute player, J. J. Quantz (1697-1773) writes about the music of the Pietà in 1746, which he considered the best of the four Ospedali and mentions a singer and organist, Angeletta, who later married a banker. Charles Burney (1726-1814) met Signora Regina Zocchi in Venice in 1770, who had been brought up at the Incurabili 'and had the advantage of being there under Hasse. She is now well married and well received everywhere she chooses to go. She is now under thirty with an agreeable figure and a pleasing countenance. She has a powerful voice and sings charmingly with great execution in allegros and expression in slow movements'.

Johann Hasse (1699-1783) was a prolific composer who settled in Venice in 1763 and composed more than 100 operas. He is remembered also for his prophecy on hearing the music of the young Mozart in 1771: 'This boy will cause us all to be forgotten.'

At the Pietà, Vivaldi had a rich store of musical ability at his disposal: his personal orchestra, as it were. The girls were clearly of exceptional ability and he improved on their natural ability to such an extent that the music of the Pietà became famous in Venice and in Italy. His association with it lasted almost forty years but was not always a peaceful or placid one. The reports of the meetings of the governors often reflect an irritation, perhaps even a certain hostility, to the brilliant violinist and composer who had added such distinction to the music of the Pietà.

While the pupils were influenced by the master, it is also true the master was influenced by his pupils, perhaps inspired by this or that instrumentalist, composing for the musical means at his disposal, which explains why Vivaldi used such a wide range of instruments and combinations of instruments. The combination of the gifted and spirited pupils of the Pietà and the gifted and furiously energetic young composer, who was only about twenty-five when he first took up his duties there, produced music that is characterised by an irrepressible energy and vitality, music which must have delighted the hearts of the young players as much as it enraptured the audience.

Vivaldi's musical output was prodigious, even in an age of prolific composers. More than 800 works have been authenticated: sonatas, sinfonias, concertos, operas, cantatas and oratorios. His contribution to the concerto form was considerable; he composed more than 450 and his composition of operatic work was on the same giant scale. He composed more than 48 and claimed to have

Johann Hasse (1699-1783) a prolific composer of operas (more than 100 to his credit) in the first half of the 18th century in Venice. Anna Girò, Vivaldi's companion, sang in operas composed by the distinguished German composer.

composed twice that number.

Such industry is breathtaking as is the breadth of the musical language employed. Most of the concertos are for one or more violins – Vivaldi was a violinist of dazzling ability, more famous for his ability as a soloist than for his compositions in his own day. These violin concertos employ many combinations of string instruments, often with the additions of flutes, oboes, horns or bassoons. There are concertos for viola d'amore, cello, flute or piccolo, bassoon, oboe.

Arcangelo Corelli (1653-1713), violinist and composer, an important figure in the history of the violin. His work provided a model for musicians of Vivaldi's time and Vivaldi's first published music, a set of trio sonatas, show the influence of Corelli.

His first published work, a collection of trio sonatas, appeared in 1705, two years after his appointment at the Pietà. They were printed in Venice by the firm of Guiseppe Sala and part of the first edition in the Venice Conservatory shows the composer described as Don Antonio Vivaldi, Musico di Violino, Professore Veneto. The trio sonata was the form for composers of the day to introduce themselves, just as a set of madrigals would have been earlier. The work in this form of the great master Corelli was an example of the possibilities of the form – Corelli (1653-1713) was the dominant influence on composers of the period, evidence of which can be seen in Vivaldi's first work as it can also in the works of the early offerings of contemporary young composers of the day such as Albinoni and Caldara, each of whom made his début with trio sonatas.

This first opus was dedicated to Count Annibale Gambara, a Venetian nobleman, with a dedication which is extremely humble even in an age when such dedications were notable for extreme humility:

My devotion, ambitious to make itself known to Your Excellency, has suffered enough from the torments of desire. I confess that many times I restrained my ardour, mindful of your merit and mistrustful of my talent, but, no longer able to contain my ambition, I thought it proper to free it from its longing, since what was earlier a mere propensity had become a necessity. When considering whether to dedicate to Your Excellency the first fruits of my feeble efforts in the form of these sonatas, I realised it was no longer in my power not to do so. Your lofty prerogatives took my judgement captive and rewarded my decision with the bounty of a Maecenas. I will not lose myself in the vast expanse of the glories of your most noble and excellent family for I would not find my way out again, since they are so immense in greatness and number. Knowing that I possess no other adornments than those of my feebleness, I have sought the patronage of a great man, who can not only protect me from the tongues of Aristarchuses and in whose shade my labours – perhaps when maligned by critics, who, in these times, like to flaunt their impertinences – can enjoy a safe refuge, but can also perform these flaccid harmonies, which with so much humility I dedicate to Your Excellency. May your exalted generosity then deign to accept in respectful tribute these first, most humble products of my labours and meanwhile grant me the honour of declaring myself the most humble, devoted and obliged servant of Your Excellency.
D. Antonio Vivaldi.

The tone is typical of the time although some commentators have detected a sensitivity towards criticism on Vivaldi's part in the reference to potential critics which is certainly sharp in tone.

His second opus went to another printer, Antonio Bortoli of Venice, was published in 1709 and was dedicated to another, much

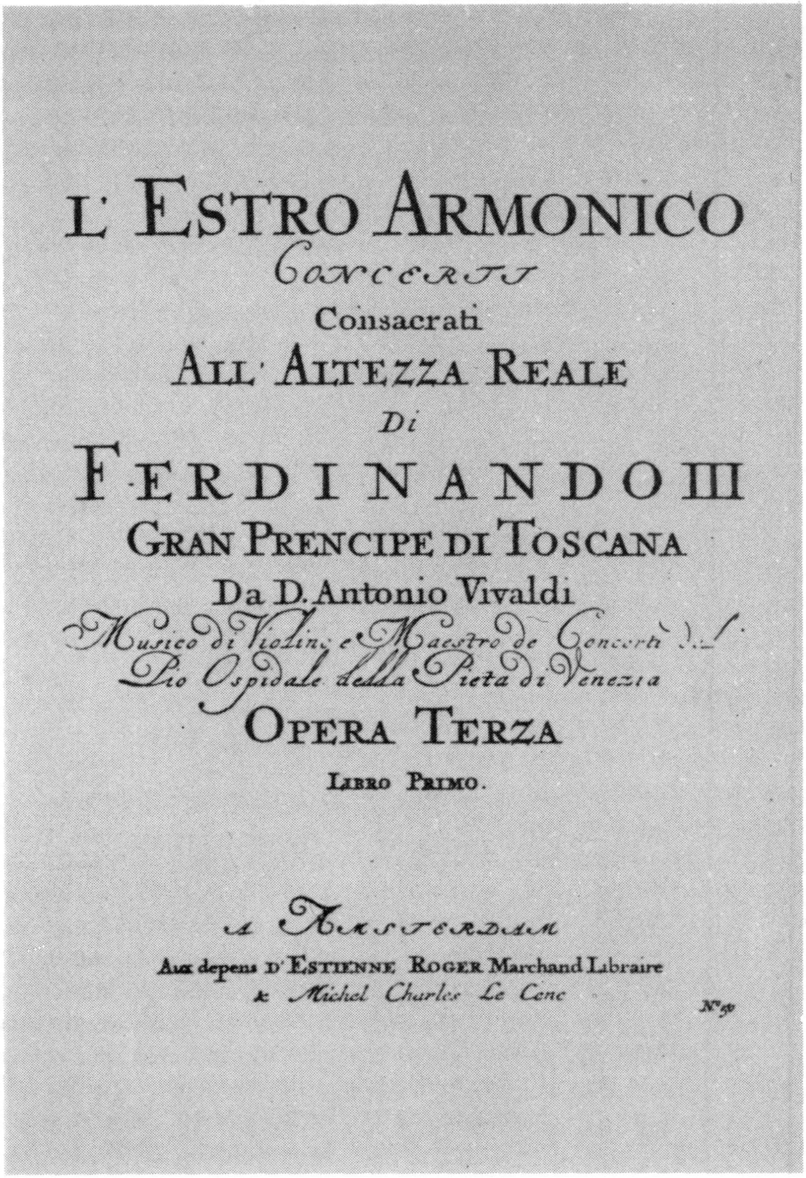

L'ESTRO ARMONICO
Concerti
Consacrati
ALL'ALTEZZA REALE
Di
FERDINANDO III
GRAN PRENCIPE DI TOSCANA
Da D. Antonio Vivaldi
Musico di Violini e Maestro de Concerti d.l.
Pio Ospidale della Pietà di Venezia
OPERA TERZA
LIBRO PRIMO.

A Amsterdam
Aux depens D'ESTIENNE ROGER Marchand Libraire
& Michel Charles Le Cene
N° 50

The title page of L'Estro Armonico, published in 1711 and dedicated to Ferdinand III of Tuscany, a work which brought Vivaldi's name before Europe.

grander nobleman, Frederick IV of Denmark and Norway (1644-77). This was of twelve sonatas for violin and harpsichord. The dedication seems to have come about by happy chance for Vivaldi because when the King paid a surprise visit to Venice in 1708-9 Gasparini was absent from his duties as musical director of the Pietà and Vivaldi deputised for him.

The King was officially incognito so he could enjoy the many pleasures of Venice but his presence was obviously widely known. He visited the Pietà on the Sunday after his arrival, as a contemporary account records:

His Majesty appeared at the Pietà at 11 o'clock after receiving ambassadors from Savoy, to hear the girls singing and playing instruments under the direction of the master who was occupying the rostrum in the absence of Gasparini. Great was the applause for the Credo and Agnus Dei that were performed with the instruments and then there was a concerto in great taste, as was appropriate.

It is possible that Vivaldi was presented to the King after the concert and it is certain that the King visited the Pietà at least once more. When he left for home on 6 March, the King was able to take the twelve sonatas dedicated to him – and portraits in miniature by Rosalba Carriera of twelve of the prettiest women in the city.

The association may have continued beyond the period of the visit. There is a substantial body of Vivaldi manuscripts in Scandinavia, as the distinguished Danish musicologist Peter Ryom has established, and it is appropriate that he, a Dane, should be responsible for the most successful and definitive cataloguing of the work of Vivaldi which has replaced former systems.

It was with the publication of Opus III, *L'estro armonico* in 1711 that Vivaldi's voice was heard throughout Europe. *L'estro armonico* – the harmonic spirit or harmonic inspiration – was a set of twelve concertos which appeared in two parts.

The work had a new dedicatee, an accomplished musician and patron of other composers such as Alessandro and Domenico Scarlatti, Albinoni and Handel, the Grand Prince Ferdinand of Tuscany (1642-1723). A new printing firm had been found, an arrangement which delighted Vivaldi, to judge from his dedication:

The kind indulgence you have so far accorded to my feeble efforts has persuaded me to seek to gratify you with a work containing instrumental concertos. I must acknowledge that if in the past my compositions have suffered from printing errors in addition to their own defects, their greatest distinction will now be that of having been engraved by the famous hand of Monsieur Estienne Roger.

A graceful tribute from the composer to the printer, and one which was sincere, because Vivaldi had his Opus I and II re-printed by Roger in Amsterdam and the same printing firm produced most of his future work. It is not known how the composer and printing firm came together although Vivaldi's contemporary, Albinoni, had his work printed by Roger, which may well have been known by Vivaldi. The printing by Roger's firm was much clearer, making the music easier to read – important in much of Vivaldi's work with its clusters of semiquavers and demisemiquavers.

With *L'estro armonico* the world became aware of a new spirit. There is a passion and urgency in the music which is quite

31

remarkable, but perhaps the most unusual feature about it is the sense of a personal voice. Vivaldi's work at this period marks a move from the polyphonic style, in which no single voice has predominance, to a style in which an individual voice comes to the forefront, against which the other voices play the role of accompaniment. Where the music of the immediate past reflected a religious background and was concerned with the group, the new music was an unashamed expression of the individual.

As the Vivaldi scholar, Marc Pincherle, author of the definitive work on Vivaldi, has commented:

He designed solos for himself that would concentrate the impassioned attention of the listener on himself as on a beloved singer at the opera, and this in the contemplative adagios still more than in the showy sections of the allegros. He glorified a personal feeling, a new lyricism, the vogue for which was as widespread as it was sudden.

The German musicologist, Alfred Einstein (1880-1952) expresses it perfectly when writing about the last movement of No. 8, Opus III:

It is as if the windows and doors of a stately baroque hall had been opened to welcome in Nature's freedom: a superb pathetic grandeur such as the 17th century had not known; a cosmopolitan's cry to the world.

Vivaldi's concertos follow the fast-slow-fast order which was the style of the time and was to remain so for many years to come, but within that order there is a wealth of invention, a dazzling display of colour and harmony. The concerto No. 10 of Opus III for four violins is one example of a concerto following the established order but exploring an intensely varied musical world. The opening allegro is powerfully engaging, contrasting with the melting lyricism of the largo which is a kind of aria of introspection, and the finale of the last movement introduces a new irrepressible energy and a brilliance of harmony that is quite breathtaking.

His skill as a violinist, a player of what must have seemed unique ability at the time, is confirmed by Johan Friedrich von Uffenbach (1687-1769) who visited Venice in February 1715 and heard Vivaldi play. Uffenbach is a valuable witness in the Vivaldi story, an architect from Frankfurt-am-Main, and more importantly, an enthusiastic musician. His description of Vivaldi's technique is illuminating:

Towards the end of the work Vivaldi performed a solo accompaniment admirably and at the end he added an improvised cadenza that quite confounded me, for such playing has not been heard before and can never be equalled. He placed his fingers but a hair's breadth from the bridge so that there was hardly room for the bow. He played thus on all four strings, with imitations and at unbelievable speed. Everyone was astonished but I cannot say that it captivated me, because it was more skilfully executed than it was pleasant to hear.

The description shows Vivaldi's skill as an innovator of technique. From von Uffenbach's evidence, Marc Pincherle, himself a violinist, deduces that he 'evolved the thirteenth, fourteenth and fifteenth positions to which, it had been believed, only Locatelli approached'. Pietro Locatelli (1695-1764) was an Italian violinist and composer, known especially as a great virtuoso who had studied with Corelli in Rome.

Burney can also be cited in support of Vivaldi's pioneering techniques: 'Geminiani used to claim the invention of the second position on the violin, and he probably brought it to England; but Italians ascribed it to Vivaldi.' Certainly Vivaldi was an incredible performer, brilliantly accomplished from the evidence of those who heard him play and from the evidence of his own work.

Pincherle finds that Vivaldi, despite his ability, or because of it, was not one of those composers who ignore the player by placing intolerable demands on his technique. The Frenchman is critical of those who attempt to impress the public by 'wheezing and sawing and other customary accessories of the cadenza'.

Vivaldi's music is not self-consciously difficult. It has a natural instinct for the best ways of achieving the best effects. While he was a genius of the violin, it should be remembered that many of the concertos he composed were performed by the young women of the Pietà who, while gifted, could not be compared with the maestro.

An interesting example of his writing for the students of the Pietà is in the concerto in F major for three violins and strings. This is a highly original work in a number of ways, apart from being the only concerto for three violins written by the composer. The slow movement is especially beautiful and is given to one violin, not the first, as might be expected, but the third, while the first and second play muted arpeggios and pizzicati. Pincherle suggests that Vivaldi composed the piece with three pupils of the Pietà in mind, and gave the slow movement to the pupil who was capable of the more beautiful tone while not being as technically accomplished as the first and second violinists. His music is popular with modern orchestral string players, probably because of this accessibility.

Chapter 3

Patrician Venice

At the time of his success in dedicating his Opus II to the King of Denmark and Norway, Vivaldi received a setback at the Pietà when the governors decided to dispense with his services. On 24 February 1709 the governors voted on his post at the Pietà. At the first vote, a majority were in favour of his retention but a further vote led to his dismissal.

Vivaldi's relationship with the authorities of the Pietà appears to have been difficult. Despite the fact that he was associated with the establishment for forty years, there was never anything comfortably secure about his employment. Even when he was a world-famous composer, honoured by princes, admired throughout Europe, the governors of the Pietà appear to have been unimpressed. To them, he was simply Don Antonio Vivaldi, whose importance lay only in his ability as a teacher to the *figli di coro* of the Pietà. There has been much speculation about their attitude towards the composer. From the beginning of his links with the Pietà, it is clear he had opponents, perhaps even enemies, and there is a distinctly wary element in their dealings with him.

Some have suggested the fault may have been in Vivaldi. He is thought to have been independent, perhaps outspoken and impatient. There is little direct evidence to support these theories which may be inspired by his music which certainly suggests a vigorous, even fiery personality. It may be that his ambition (for example, the way in which he seized the opportunity to make an impression on the royal visitor to the Pietà during Gasparini's absence) irritated the governors. As time went on, his increasing commitments outside the Pietà may well have made them feel he could not entirely fulfil his obligations to the Pietà. On the other hand, it may simply have been a patrician attitude towards an employee. Venice was a state of rigid social structure. All political power was in the hands of the nobility; a group of aristocratic families who were listed in the Golden Book, the patrician families of the city state. Power evolved from this patrician group to the Council of Ten and then to the even more exclusive Council of Three, a group which was elected monthly. At the head of the state was the elected doge, which was a non-hereditary position.

The effect and purpose of this form of government was to reduce the possibilities of personal power on the part of any individual. In Venice, the state was ruthless in protecting its own interests. Although Venice had many churches, the church was firmly separated from power. 'Venetians first, Christians afterwards' was the saying. All priests had to be Venetians and bishops were nominated in the Senate.

The patrician families of the Golden Book were as much the servants of the Republic as the common people. No one, not even the most noble, could leave Venice without permission. The state governed completely, decreeing what its patricians should wear, for example, and expected them to accept any appointment that might be offered. The lower classes had no power and no expectation of any. If the winds of freedom and revolution were stirring elsewhere in Europe, they did not cross the Adriatic.

Venice did not approve the cult of the individual. Indeed, anyone who loomed too large on the Venetian stage was in danger of being regarded as a threat to the state. A victorious commander was as likely to be prosecuted as honoured, as in the case of Antonio da Lezze, for example, who performed heroically against the Turks at Soutari. He defended the place for almost a year but finally had to surrender and returned to Venice. There no honours were heaped upon him; he was charged with treason and banished for ten years from the Republic. Failure and success were twin imposters in the Republic and each might receive the same treatment.

Against this background it is possible that the governors of the Pietà, being patricians, would have taken an autocratic line with an employee, however distinguished he might be in his own sphere. The concept of the artist as an individual had not yet developed. A composer or painter was simply a person providing a service, in the same way as a blacksmith or manservant.

There are many statues in Venice today but most of them date from the 19th century. In the days of the republic there were few monuments to individuals: the city was celebration enough. The scarcity of information about Vivaldi might be explained by this suspicion of the individual. There are many examples of contemporary Venetians about whom little is known – Canaletto, the painter, is as shadowy as Vivaldi, despite the fame he enjoyed in his life; and there is a similar lack of information about the composer Tomaso Albinoni (1671-1751). Expert opinion is that the two composers did not know each other, which seems quite

Francesco Gasparini (1668-1727), maestro di coro at the Pietà from 1700 to 1713 who was succeeded by Vivaldi. It was probably as a result of his request for a violin teacher that Vivaldi was first appointed at the Pietà.

incredible. Albinoni was born in Venice and came from a wealthy family of paper makers. He was not a member of any of the musical establishments of Venice and had no connections with San Marco or any of the Ospedali. Because he came from a wealthy family, he had no need to become a professional musician and composed for his own pleasure; but his musical output is considerable and includes operas, cantatas, sonatas and concertos. Like Vivaldi, he enjoys considerable popularity today although he is considered a lesser figure than *Il Prete Rosso*. In two respects they might have met – they had the same publisher, Roger of Amsterdam, and the operatic singer, Anna Girò, with whom Vivaldi was closely associated, made her début in an Albinoni opera.

So far as Vivaldi is concerned, although he has been restored to favour in Venice, there is little public recognition of his existence. His name is inextricably associated with the city and he is regarded as one of its favourite sons but there is a possibility that the recognition has been prompted by commercial rather than musical considerations. True, concerts of his music are performed regularly in the church of the Pietà on the Riva degli Schiavoni and there is a modest plaque on the side of the church which the observant visitor might spot, but that is all. There is certainly no cult of the composer, a situation the governors of the 18th-century Pietà would have considered seemly.

A simple inscription on the wall of La Pietà records Antonio Vivaldi's connection with the Ospedale della Pietà as *maestro de concerti*.

Chapter 4

Opera

Little is known about Vivaldi's activities during the short period he was absent from the Pietà. There has been speculation that he might have visited Holland to see the publisher Roger or have made a visit to Florence, but there is no evidence of either journey.

It is likely that he performed as a violinist for distinguished visitors and in the theatre as his father did. It may be that he was performing the concertos of Opus III, *L'estro armonico*, during this period since there is some evidence to support the theory that the work was written well before the publication date of 1711.

It is certain that he would have been involved in, and drawn to, the chief musical passion of Venice: opera. The birth of opera can be placed at Mantua on 24 January 1607, when Monteverdi's (1567-1643) *Orfeo* was first performed. The ruling family of Mantua were the Gonzagas whose court was famous for its music, painting and poetry.

The first public opera house in Europe, the San Cassiano, was opened in Venice in 1637. This, as were most of them, was owned by a patrician family. M. Chassebras de Cramailles writes about the Venetian opera in the 17th century:

There are in Venice eight theatres, which take their names from the churches nearest to the places where they are erected. Almost all of them belong to Venetian nobles who had them built or have them by inheritance. The small ones are rented by troupes of comedians who betake themselves to Venice from the month of November on; and the large ones are reserved for the operas that are ordered and paid for by these nobles or others. But it is rather for their entertainment than for their profit, because they do not take in enough to defray the cost.

The San Cassiano was owned by the Tron family; the Santi Giovanni e Paolo by the Grimani, who also owned the San Giovanni Cristostomo and the San Samuele; while the San Moisè was owned by the distinguished Giustiniani family (said to be descendants

of the emperor Justinian), and San Salvatore by the Vendramin family. It became the fashion and a matter of social prestige for these noble families to be associated with a theatre providing the best entertainment.

The Venetians took an immediate liking to opera and more theatres were opened to cater for the public demand which was almost insatiable; operas were composed, performed and often discarded at an alarming rate. Pincherle estimates there were 150 operas performed between 1680 and 1700 by composers such as Caldara, Albinoni, Lotti and Legrenzi; 432 between 1700 and 1743 by masters such as Galuppi, Hasse, Alessandro Scarlatti and Gluck. Such industry is staggering by modern standards as the German musicologist Walter Kolneder points out. He compares these figures with a modern operatic repertoire of about 60 works and cites the example of Carlo Francesco Pollarolo (1653-1722) who wrote 70 operas between 1685 and 1722, an average of two a year, in addition to his other musical duties which were by no means trivial – organist at San Marco and *maestro di cappella* and teacher at the Ospedali degli Incurabili. Operatic output on such a scale was common. Antonio Caldara produced more than 60 operas (1670-1736): Baldassare Galuppi wrote more than 112 (1706-85); Johann Hasse (1699-1783) wrote more than 100; Vivaldi's superior at the Pietà, Francesco Gasparini, was also a prolific composer.

The Venetian passion for opera was shared by visitors to the city who have left many eye-witness accounts. John Evelyn records his impressions of a visit in 1645:

This night, having with my Lord Bruce taken our places before, we went to the Opera, where comedies and other plays are represented in recitative music, by the most excellent musicians, vocal and instrumental, with variety of scenes painted and contrived with no less art of perspective, and machines for flying in the air, and other wonderful notions; taken together it is one of the most magnificent and expensive diversions the wit of man can invent. The history was, Hercules in Lydia; the scenes changed thirteen times. The famous voices, Anna Rencia, a Roman, and reputed the best treble of women; but there was an eunuch who, in my opinion, surpassed her; also a Genoese that sung an incomparable bass.

The sumptuous interior of the ducal palace at Mantua which may well have been known to Vivaldi. Mantua had a long history as a centre of the arts which reached a peak under the Gonzaga family, who ruled the duchy in great splendour before it became part of the Austrian Empire.

The Venetian love of entertainment found full expression in opera. The form combined their twin delights, spectacle and music. The sets for these operas were extraordinary with remarkable lighting and stage machinery. One set in glass represented the temple of Saturn and had three storeys with stairways, balconies and statues. It was lit from inside and evidently to brilliant effect. There were mechanical camels and elephants, also live horses. Little wonder that the civilised world marvelled at these breathtaking effects and news of them spread throughout Europe.

Something of the tradition continues even today as a visit to opera at the Fenice theatre, close to the Piazza of San Marco, will illustrate.

The operatic world of the early 18th century was very different from the world of opera as it is known today at Covent Garden or even La Scala. The pious, respectful approach of the modern opera-lover would have seemed strange to the Venetian of the 18th century. Opera was entertainment, a diversion, a lighthearted way of spending an evening. Long runs were unknown. When Handel's *Agrippina* was performed in 1709 it was a sensation, a fact underlined by the fact that it enjoyed a run of some seventeen successive performances. An opera was an ephemeral thing, produced, enjoyed and put aside, and the approach to the entertainment explains the huge number of operas composed and presented and the superficial nature of many of them.

George Frederick Handel (1685-1759) whose opera Agrippina was performed in Venice in 1709 and had enormous success—which could hardly have escaped the notice of the Red Priest.

Johann Friedrich Armand von Uffenbach (1687-1749) is an invaluable source on operas in general and on Vivaldi in particular. When he arrived in Venice on 2 February 1715, from his home in Frankfurt-am-Main, his first thought was to go to the opera. He was astonished when he saw what he had been longing to see. He chose to visit one of the largest, the Santi Giovannie e Paolo where he saw a performance of what was probably Pollarolo's *Marsia deluso*. His first impressions were not of the opera but of the audience. The atmosphere was like a gaming house or tavern with people talking, playing cards and generally showing no attention to the work being performed. Worse, in the experience of the distinguished visitor, was the loutish behaviour of many of the audience. Seats had recently been introduced to the opera houses and he had managed to obtain one in what we would call the stalls. Unfortunately, the people in the stalls were the target

Gambling was one of the Venetian passions and ridotti or gambling salons were as popular as theatres. The painting, Le Ridotto, is by Pietro Longhi, a contemporary of Vivaldi.

of the people in the upper areas and were assaulted with apple cores and orange peel and spat on – von Uffenbach recalls 'a revolting gob' landing on the libretto he was holding.

Gambling was another Venetian passion and one which was associated with the theatres. John Evelyn describes a visit to the opera in 1645 which ended at two in the morning when 'we went to the Chetto de san Felice, to see the noblemen and their ladies at bassett, a game of cards which is much used'.

There were three opera seasons in Venice. The principal one was the winter Carnival from 26 December to 30 March; the lesser two were the Spring season from Whit Monday to 30 June and the Autumn season from 1 September to 30 November. The ever

An engraving of Venice during the Carnival, a time of mad pleasure in the Republic, which attracted fascinated visitors from the rest of Europe.

observant John Evelyn has painted a graphic picture of the Carnival during the 17th century when he wrote of Shrovetide:

. . . all the world repairs to Venice, to see the folly and madness of the Carnival: the women, men and persons of all conditions disguising themselves in antique dresses, with extravagant music and a thousand gambols, traversing the streets from house to house, all places being accessible and free to enter. Abroad, they fling eggs filled with sweet water but sometimes not oversweet. They also have a barbarous custom of hunting bulls about the streets and piazzas, which is very dangerous, the passages being generally narrow. The youth of several wards and parishes contend in other masteries and pastimes, so that it is impossible to recount the universal madness of this place during this time of licence. The great banks are set up for those who will play at bassett; the comedians have liberty, and the operas are open; witty pasquils are thrown about, and the mountebanks have their stages at every corner.

Masks were worn during Carnival which were intended to give anonymity to the wearers. Patricians and commoners would mingle as equals for the brief madness of Carnival – and madness it seems to have been. Certainly visitors were aware of, and attracted by, the sense of uninhibited freedom that swept through the city. Edward Wright in the 1720s speaks of the 'sort of frenzy or madness' which gripped the people of Venice from the beginning of the New Year.

Von Uffenbach's first experience of the Venetian opera did not discourage him. On 4 February 1715 he returned, as he reports in his diary:

I went with several acquaintances to the Teatro San Angelo, which was smaller but also not so costly as the one I have described above. Its impresario was the famous Vivaldi, who has composed the opera, which was very fine and pleasing to see. The machinery was not so elaborate as in the other theatre; the orchestra was not so strong, but no less worthy of being listened to. In fear of being mistreated and spat upon as in the big opera houses, we took a loge (it was not very costly) and revenged ourselves in the local fashion upon the parterre just as had been done to us the previous time, which struck me as almost impossible. The singers were incomparable and yielded nothing to those of the big opera house, especially certain of the women; of these, the so-called Fabri

Masks were a common feature in Venetian society, especially during the Carnival when the masks gave anonymity during the reckless round of pleasure. This painting shows masked figures in a Venetian palace by Longhi.

excelled as much in musicianship as in charm. Moreover, she was very beautiful; at least she appeared so on the stage.

The women of Venice, not only the courtesans, were judged to be one of the city's adornments. It is worth noting that red hair, like Vivaldi's, was not uncommon as the Venetians were not, and are not, of the dark Latin type. The blood of the Slavs, the Hungarians and the Austrians had mingled with them producing a distinctive cast of features and colouring. In the paintings of the great Venetian masters can be seen the characteristic Venetian look: auburn hair and pale complexions. They had Latin appetites, however, as is recalled by Mrs Thrale who is more widely known for her association with Doctor Johnson than as an authority on Venetian mores, but is a valuable guide as she married an Italian after her friendship with the great man and wrote at length about her travels in Italy. She said of the ladies of Venice, perhaps a little complacently:

Like all sensualists, however, they fail of the end proposed from hurry to obtain it; and consume those charms which alone can procure them continuance or change of admirers; they injure their health too irreparably, and that in their earliest youth; for few remain unmarried till fifteen, and at thirty they have a wan and faded look. *On ne goûte pas ses plaisirs ici, on les avale* (they do not taste their pleasures here, they swallow them whole) said Madame la Présidente yesterday, very judiciously.

They are sentiments the good doctor might have approved but it would be interesting to hear what Lord Byron, who startled even Venice with his reckless behaviour, might have said.

Vivaldi was re-appointed at the Pietà in September 1711 as a violin teacher, evidently in recognition of his talents as a teacher and of the need to provide the talented pupils with expert tuition. This time the governors were unanimous that he should be appointed at an annual salary of 60 ducats 'being certain that he will exercise his talent to the utmost in the good service of this pious establishment, and for the greatest profit of those girls'.

The need for a teacher of real ability was necessary because some of the girls were extremely talented. In order to advance they needed the finest tuition available and there was also the musical reputation of the Ospedali. De Brosses thought Chiaretta of the Pietà the best violinist in Italy, a tribute paid by Von Poellnitz to Anna Maria of the same establishment a few years earlier.

Vivaldi was in favour at the Pietà and his appointment was confirmed in the years 1712 and 1713. The year 1713 was a momentous one for the composer who was then thirty-five. This was the year of his first opera, *Ottone in Villa*, which received its first performance not in Venice but in nearby Vicenza. Vivaldi would have been familiar with opera from his earliest days, like all good Venetians, and probably had more direct experience from playing in theatre orchestras. As it was the musical form most in demand, it is natural that he should have wanted to compose for it, and it is clear he was temperamentally drawn to theatrical music.

There was nothing odd in a priest being concerned with opera. Worldly priests were common enough in every sphere of activity and there are parallels in music for Vivaldi. Landi's opera *Il San Alessio* of 1632 was to a libretto by a future Pope, Clement IX; Daniele Castrovillari, who composed operas between 1660 and 1662, was a Franciscan; and Cardinal Grimani was responsible for the libretto of Handel's great success, *Agrippina* which was performed in Venice in 1709.

Perhaps Vivaldi chose Vicenza for his début as an operatic composer because it was not the fiercely competitive world of Venice, or it may be he was allowed the opportunity, as a beginner, to try his skills away from the mainstream of the city. The first performance at the Teatro della Grazie on 17 March 1713 was evidently successful and marked the appearance of a major operatic force. The libretto was by an interesting minor character, Domenico Lalli, whose real name was Sebastiano Biancardi who had fled from his home town of Naples under a cloud, having been accused of embezzlement from his employer, the Bank of the Annunciation. He arrived in Venice in 1710 and became established as a popular librettist, collaborating with Vivaldi in a number of operas and working with other composers of the day such as Alessandro Scarlatti.

Another event of significance in that year, 1713, was the departure of Gasparini who was granted permission to leave his post and Venice on the grounds of ill health. He never returned to Venice but flourished in the musical climate of Rome where he was highly successful, becoming *maestro di cappella* at St John Lateran.

A number of appointments were made to replace Gasparini but Vivaldi does not appear to have been thought worthy of the post. The new appointments were unsuccessful, however, and Vivaldi was given the task of providing compositions which was a major part of the maestro's duties. In June 1715 the governors discussed the question of these compositions.

Having noted from the petition of the Reverend Don Antonio Vivaldi, violin master in this pious establishment, and the deposition of the officers in charge of music just read out, the acknowledged services and well-rewarded labours performed by him, not only in the successful and universally approved teaching of musical instruments to the girls, but also the excellent musical compositions supplied after the departure of

A tiny square behind the church of La Pietà, little changed since the time of Vivaldi.

45

the above-mentioned maestro Gasparini – a complete Mass, a Vespers, an oratorio, over 30 motets and other works – and seeing fit in its generosity to give him a token of its gratitude and recompense him in part for these services outside his normal duties, resolves that a single payment of 50 ducats be made to him from our exchequer in appreciation of his efforts and special contributions. And may this also stimulate him to make further contributions and to perfect still more the performing abilities of the girls of this our orchestra, so necessary to the musical standards of, and the good reputation of, this our chapel.

Only two governors were against the motion on this occasion but it is possible to suppose there was more to the matter than the calm prose of the report reveals, and indicates Vivaldi had petitioned the governors on the matter, drawing their attention to the number of compositions he had provided without additional financial reward and they, after careful deliberation, noting that his labours are 'well rewarded' before granting an extra payment.

That year, shortly after the performance of his first opera, Vivaldi

The ducal palace at Mantua. Vivaldi spent three years at Mantua in the service of Prince Philip of Darmstadt, the cultivated governor of the province. It seems likely that the period Vivaldi was in the service of the prince was 1718-20: his opera La Candace o siano was first performed there in 1720.

was granted leave for a month by the governors of the Pietà to exercise his skills beyond the city, as the records put it. Some biographers pinpoint this time as the beginning of a period of service with the Prince of Darmstadt, Philip of Hesse-Darmstadt, who was governor of Mantua in 1707-8 and 1714-35. This is the 'very devout prince' referred to by Vivaldi in his letter of 16 November 1737 in which he says he had been in his service at Mantua for three years. Marc Pincherle puts forward a convincing hypothesis that his period in the service of Philip of Darmstadt was in the period 1720-23. Kolnedor favours 1719-22 and Peter Ryom agrees with him.

As we have seen, the world of Venetian – or, indeed, Italian – opera was far removed from that of later times when the composer was the undisputed master of the creation. In Vivaldi's day, the composer was well down in the order of things, below the singers who were the principal attraction. The music was intended to show off the talents of the singers and the plots of the operas were not intended to engage too much attention. The operas had a set form which made them easy to write and they were frantically dashed off to satisfy the urgent public demand. Vivaldi, like other composers, rewrote from his own works and borrowed freely from other composers. The composers may have been unhappy with their position but it was the fashion of the times.

A treatise of 1715 sounds a sardonic note when advising composers:

Be resigned to the exchanging of your good arias for bad ones if some singer wants to add one of your recitatives which had brought him or her applause in Milan, Genoa, Venice or elsewhere. Though it may express the opposite sentiment to what is required, do not let this grieve you. Let them insert it, else you will have them all after you, sopranos and altos bearing down on you with their complaints. The librettist has to find out the impresario's intentions, that is, how many changes of scenery he has ordered for the painter; whether he has ordered any machines from the stage engineer, and how many costumes his wardrobe contains . . . how small the stage is, and how stingy the manager might be.

The composer had a struggle to win the attention of audiences. Singers were the darlings of the time and their wishes dominated the way the operas were written. People went to the opera to meet friends, for uninhibited enjoyment. They chatted loudly, smoked, ate and drank, gambled, even talked to their favourite singers when they were not engaged in the business of the opera.

The recitatives were long and rambling, often incomprehensible, but they were not usually listened to, serving as a pause between

47

This statue of Carlo Goldoni (1707-93) stands in Campo San Bartolomeo in Venice. Goldoni's fame rests on his comedies but he wrote several librettos, including some for Vivaldi's operas. Much of our information about Vivaldi comes from descriptions of the composer in Goldoni's *Mémoires* which appeared in Paris in 1787 and are especially valuable because Goldoni had first-hand information about Vivaldi.

arias. The rules were quite rigid, and composer and librettist would be left in no doubt what was required of them in the way of arias to show off the ability of particular singers and to ensure that stars of lesser rank were not presented with opportunities to outshine their superiors.

Carlo Goldoni (1707-93) in his *Mémoires* describes his early experience with the world of Venetian opera and the advice he was given:

But here one must begin by pleasing the actors and actresses; one must satisfy the composer of the music; one must consult the painter-decorator; there are rules for everything and it would be a crime of lèse-playwrighting if one infringed them. The three principal characters in the play must sing five arias each; two in the first act, two in the second and one in the third. The second actress and the second male lead may only have three arias and the least characters must be content with one or two at the very most. The author of the words must provide the musician with the different nuances that form the light and shade of the music, and make sure that two pathetic arias do not occur together. With the same precaution the bravura arias must be shared out, the action arias, the demi-character arias and minuets and rondos. Above all, extreme care must be taken not to give passionate arias, nor bravura arias, nor rondos, to second rank characters.

The singers demanded, and received, extraordinarily high fees, rather as modern stars do, the prestige of the singer increasing according to the money paid for his or her services. They often had clear ideas of how they should appear before their public. The castrato, Luigi Marchesi, liked to make his entrance on top of a hill, accoutred with sword, shield, and lance and wearing a plumed helmet, whatever the circumstances of the opera.

The *castrati* were popular and powerful in the operatic world but were not universally admired by visitors. Joseph Addison, who was in Venice in 1701-3, observed:

Operas are another great entertainment of this season. The poetry of them is generally as exquisitely ill as the music is good. The arguments are often taken from some celebrated action of the ancient Greeks or Romans, which sometimes looks ridiculous enough, for who can endure to hear one of the rough old Romans speaking through the mouth of an eunuch especially when they may chuse *(sic)* a subject out of courts where eunuchs are really actors, or represent by them any of the soft Asiatic monarchs?

The Frenchman, Misson, was equally dismissive, speaking of:

Those unhappy men who basely suffer themselves to be maimed, that they may have the finer voices. The silly figure, which in my opinion such a mutilated figure makes, one who at times acts the bully and sometimes the passionate lover, with his effeminate voice and wrinkled face, is not to be endured.

Yet the *castrato* stars were hugely popular in general, which suggests Addison and Misson were out of sympathy with the taste of the time.

Opera, in any event, requires a suspension of strictly rational intellectual faculties and a willingness to take part in make-believe, which the Venetian audiences were clearly capable of doing. They accepted the extraordinary plots, the amazing coincidences, the fearsome creatures which appeared and were slain by the intrepid heroes, *castrati* or not. The singers were paramount, often introducing themselves with a favoured aria and putting themselves firmly centre stage throughout the proceedings. A typical scene is reported in respect of the opera *Il sacrifice di Greta* by Peter Von Winter in 1712, in which the tenor, playing Theseus, bravely slays the Minotaur while ending his bravura aria. The aria was greeted with loud applause and calls for an encore so it was repeated with the Minotaur coming to life again to enliven the stage before being despatched for a second time.

An illustration of the value of the composer in the operatic scheme of things has been discovered by Walter Kolneder who pointed out that in 1725 at the Hamburg opera 100 florins was spent on providing the principal actor's helmet while the composer received 50 for the score.

However, Vivaldi was committed to the form, and works flooded from him. The first opera at Vicenza, *Ottone in Villa*, was successful and news of its success was not unremarked upon in Venice where rival impresarios were eager for new talent. His next opera, *Orlando finto pazzo*, saw his début in Venice as a composer of operas, at the S. Angelo Teatro in 1714, an association which was to last until the end of his operatic career. The new opera had a new librettist, Dottor Grazio Braccioli, and was dedicated to the General of the Imperial Infantry, the Margrave of Baden – it was common in the period for the librettist to present a copy of the libretto to a distinguished person.

Particularly interesting is the introduction to the general reader, outlining the plot and giving the cast:

Orlando – Mr A. F. C., singer at the court of Her Serene Highness the Grand Duchesse Violante of Tuscany; Ersilia, Fair Queen, called Falerina by the Boyards, loves Brandimarte and Origille, thought to be Oradauro. Miss M. G., called C: Tigrina – loves Artillano. Miss E. D; Origille – loves Grifone, pretends to be a man named Oradauro. Miss A. M. F.: Argillana – chosen warrior of Ersilia and in love with her. Mr A. P. Grifone – loves Tigrinda, pretends to be a woman named

Leodilla. Mr F. N. – Brandimarte – friend of Orlando, loved by Ersilia, gives out to be Orlando.

The following year, 1715, Vivaldi produced *nerone fatto Cesare* for the S. Angelo, although the work was by a number of composers with Vivaldi providing twelve arias.

More operas followed; the furiously energetic Vivaldi producing operas with the same speed as he produced instrumental works. *La costanza trionfante degl'amori e degl'odi* was given at the S. Angelo in 1716 and two further works, *Arsilda, regina di Ponto* and *L'incoronazione di Dario*, were given at the same theatre in the same year.

From the records we know that Vivaldi averaged almost two operas a year in the period 1713-39; an output that was to win admiration and to attract criticism.

Vivaldi quickly became involved in the productions of his operas, and of some others, as impresario. Because of the lowly status of the composer, it was necessary for a composer who wished to

The parish church of San Martino with which Vivaldi and his family were associated. His father, Giovanni Vivaldi, became a leading violinist in Venice and was a founder member of a musical society, *Sovvegno dei musicisti di Santa Cecilia*, which was based at the church.

maintain control over his work to become an impresario. Handel did the same thing, for the same reasons. As early as 1715 one report describes Vivaldi as the impresario. The work of management covered a wide range of tasks from selling tickets to recruiting the singers and dancers in the company and, of course, negotiating payments with them. It was hard, frustrating and demanding work which again gives the lie to the portrait of Vivaldi, painted by himself in his letters to Bentivoglio, of a sick man, almost housebound.

There was, too, a shadowy side to the world of opera. Morals in the world of opera, with singers and protectors, disputes about money, were sometimes dubious. Violence was not unknown. There is a story that Saturnini, impresario at the S. Angelo theatre, arranged for singers engaged in Gasparini's *Tiberio imperatore d'Oriente* to be beaten after they attempted to leave the city, claiming they had not been paid for their services. Vivaldi probably knew Saturnini, as the impresario also lived in the district of S. Martino, and might also have met him through his own or his father's connections with the theatre. His father's involvement with S. Angelo was not only musical, although he played there, but was also financial, as the records of a long legal wrangle about the theatre show.

Saturnini had been granted a limited lease of the land on which he built the S. Angelo and appears to have refused to return the land when the lease ended. Among the papers in the case when the legal owners were suing for the return of their property is one which lists a number of debtors, including Giovanni Battista, Vivaldi's father. It was clearly a world of high emotions – charges and counter charges, likely to explode into violence – as it did in 1713 when the poet Bartolomeo Dotti was killed in mysterious circumstances.

The San Samuele theatre in Venice, one of a number of magnificent theatres which flourished during Vivaldi's lifetime when there was a huge appetite for opera. Vivaldi's Griselda had its first performance there in 1735.

Chapter 5

A Musical Laboratory

To be able to survive in the world of operatic management, to say nothing of operatic music, required resilience and energy, qualities which Vivaldi evidently possessed. In contrast to this world was the Pietà, with which he was still closely connected. His first oratorio *Moyses Deus Pharaonis* was performed in 1714 at the Pietà. Unfortunately only the libretto remains, but it is of great interest, showing that all the parts were sung by female voices, as would be expected at the Pietà. The cast was large; there are three choruses of Jews, Egyptians and Jewish women as well as the principals who are listed as:

Moyses, Barbara; Aron, Candida; Elysabeth Aaron Uxor, Silvia; Maria sorer Moysis et Aaron, Michielina; Pharao Egypti Rex, Anastasia; Sapens primus, Soprano. As with the instrumentalists, the girls of the Pietà were known only by their Christian names

The first page of Juditha Triumphans performed at the Pietà in 1716.

52

or even only as 'soprano'. In 1716 Vivaldi's second oratorio, *Juditha triumphans*, was presented at the Pietà. This was a great success and is regarded as a masterpiece, especially for its use of instrumental colouring. Vivaldi always employed a wide range of instruments, seizing anything to hand in his urge to explore and expand the musical possibilities. An example used in this oratorio is the salmoè, already rare in Vivaldi's time, which has intrigued musicologists. Pincherle was not sure what the instrument was and thought it might be a type of clarinet but Kolneder argues that it was more likely to be a shawn, a double-reeded predecessor of the oboe. *Clareni,* or clarinets, and *trombe,* or trumpets, are also indicated in the work.

The instruments used in the work were recorders, oboes, salmoè, clarinets, bassoons, trumpets, timpani, mandolin, theorbos, viola d'amore, viola da gamba, violins, viola, cello, double bass, harpsichords and organ. The instruments are used with great skill in the dramatic interpretation of the plot and the range gives some idea of the variety of musical skills available at the Pietà.

The work was an allegory of Venice's struggles against the mighty Turks. Although Venice was declining as a great power, she still had the trappings of greatness and there were occasions when the state's fortunes seemed to be thriving again as in this year, when the Venetians were successful in winning Corfu from the Turkish armies and restoring the colony to Venice again. The Venetians were proudly patriotic and Vivaldi was a Venetian.

The oratorio is set in the year 659 BC and concerns the story of Judith and Holofernes. The latter is a soldier, sent by Nebuchadnezzar to punish a rebellious group of Jews. Juditha, beautiful widow, appeals for mercy for the beleaguered town of Bethulia, and Holofernes, listening to her, is aroused to love and invites her to his tent so he can pursue his ardour. But he falls asleep, Judith beheads him and the town is saved. The message of the work is made clear when the high priest sings of the freed town:

Rejoice, happy Bethulia, comfort thee, thou hard-tried city, thou art loved of heaven, fortune, unvanquished in the midst of foes.

The fate of Bethulia is then likened to that of Venice:

Thus I see, by eternal decree, Venice, city of the sea, inviolate. Just as in Asia, against the heathen tyrant Holofernes, the virginal city, always protected by God's grace, will be a new Judith . . .

The governors of the Pietà were apparently not entirely convinced about their virtuoso composer-teacher and the records

The title page of Juditha Triumphans, which is described as a sacred military oratorio. It is an allegory about the struggle for power between the Venetian and Turkish empires and was performed at a time when the Venetians were victorious, an event which no doubt helped the success of the work.

of the Pietà continue to reflect an element of concern in their dealings with him. In 1716 they deliberated once more about his employment with the Pietà and a ballot on his future was less than the required two-thirds in his favour. A further ballot even lost him one vote, but there were second thoughts and he was reinstated with the title of *maestro di coro*.

The performance of the brilliant *Juditha triumphans* at the Pietà may have followed from his successful appointment – he was reinstated in May and the oratorio performed in November – or the composition of this 'sacred military oratorio' may have been known to the govenors at the times of their deliberations.

The duties of musical directors of the Ospedali were considerable. At the Pietà, for example, they included two new Masses and vespers for Easter and the Feast of the Visitation of the Blessed Virgin Mary, at least two new motets each month,

and any other compositions ordered in Holy Week.
The *maestro di coro* had to be present:

. . . in the choir at all the main Feast-days and especially at Easter, at Christmas, at the Feast of the Visitation, and during Holy Week, and

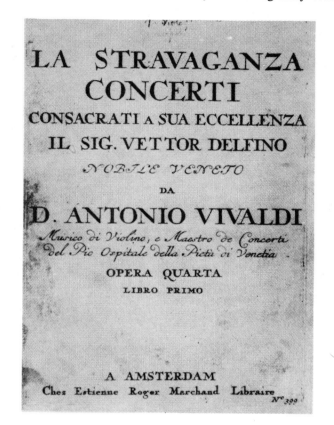

La Stravaganza, Vivaldi's Opus IV, a collection of concertos for violin published in Amsterdam in 1714.

in cases of funeral ceremonies, to play the organ and supervise the instruments and performance, so that he can give instructions to the girls, and in any other case according to the directions of the aforesaid men appointed to direct the church. He must leave copies of scores to the principal choir girl who will attend to them without any burden on the maestro.

This information is revealing as it shows that the Pietà ensured that it had the right to keep control over all music composed in its service. It also shows something of the status of the senior girls as an earlier reference says 'these compositions must be entered in the register of the principal choirgirl so that it can be examined at the assembly of church directors every six months'.

It seems likely that Vivaldi assisted with compositions during Gasparini's illness and we know he provided music from 1713 after

Gasparini's departure on the grounds of ill-health. The governors were demanding masters, jealous of the establishment's reputation. It may have seemed to them that a man with such wide musical interests as Vivaldi could not give enough of his time to the work of the Pietà, and such suspicions were confirmed by his later absences from the establishment on lengthy foreign journeys.

Vivaldi, however, was more than a church composer. His instrumental music was known throughout Europe; *L'estro armonico* had made his name known wherever music was played. He continued to explore the potential of instrumental music, producing twelve concertos for strings in 1714 which were titled *La stravaganza* and dedicated to a young Venetian nobleman, Vettor Delfino, to whom he had given violin tuition. Opus IV – a collection of four sonatas for violin and continuo, and two trio sonatas – was published in Amsterdam in 1716 by the firm of Roger, which was now under the control of Jeanne Roger, the owner's daughter.

There has been some speculation about why Vivaldi continued his association with the Pietà. He was famous, successful, able to offer himself for any of the leading musical posts in Italy or beyond. Furthermore, he seems to have been an independent, assertive personality, probably uncomfortable under the autocratic control of the Pietà. One explanation is that at the Pietà Vivaldi had his own musical laboratory, much as Haydn at Esterháza. We know about the relaxed world of the theatre, we have the vivid descriptions of the manners of the time, of the gambling, talking, against which the music struggled for attention.

At the Pietà the music was the glory of the establishment, the focus of all attention. The singers and instrumentalists were at his bidding, eager to do their utmost for their musical director. The contrast between these ardent, youthful girls and the divisive, competitive world of opera must have been striking.

Chapter 6

The Man

While there is an open approachable style about Vivaldi the composer, there is an elusive element about Vivaldi the man. He rarely speaks for himself, apart from the letters to Bentivoglio, which are about a particular matter and only inform us about his feelings on that matter, and the occasional additional written reference on some of the manuscripts. For the rest, he is glimpsed briefly through the eyes of others, a shadowy figure seen as a character of greater or lesser importance in the stories of other men. There is something frustrating in even the most valuable of these eye-witness accounts as fascinating personal snippets of information are revealed – how Vivaldi spoke, his manner of talking, the minutia from which a full portrait can be made – but which prompt more questions which remain unanswered.

Robert Browning, that adopted son of Venice, who died there in Ca' Rezzonico on the Grand Canal in 1889 echoes that feeling of longing and frustration in his lines about a quite different individual:

> Ah, did you once see Shelley plain,
> And did he stop and speak to you,
> And did you talk to him again –
> How strange it seems and new.

There is something of that sense when reading the accounts of those who saw and spoke to Vivaldi. One of the most valuable of these is from Johann Friedrich von Uffenbach from Frankfurt-am-Main, who was in Venice in 1715 where he was inspired to meet Vivaldi after hearing his music at the opera. We have seen from his account of a visit to the S. Angelo on 4 February the impression the brilliant playing of Vivaldi made on him. He also reveals how deeply involved the composer was in the production of the opera, composing, conducting and playing a solo accompaniment.

A plaque on the wall of the Ca' Rezzonico remembers Robert Browning who died there in the 19th century. The inscription is the poet's couplet: 'Open my heart and you will see, Graven inside of it, Italy.'

Later in the month von Uffenbach returned to the theatre for another opera by Vivaldi which did not please him as much, perhaps because 'Vivaldi himself played solo on the violin only a very slight aria'. A following visit delighted him, however, especially the virtuoso playing of the maestro. He determined to make the acquaintance of the composer and made several attempts to do so. At last he was successful, as he records in his diary for Wednesday, 6 March 1715:

After dinner Vivaldi, the famous composer and violinist, came to my home, for I had sent invitations to him a number of times. I spoke of some concerti grossi that I would like to have from him, and I ordered them from him. For him, since he belonged to the *Cantores*, some bottles of wine were ordered. He then let me hear some very difficult and quite inimitable improvisations on the violin. From close to, I had to admire his skill all the more, and I saw quite clearly that he played unusual and lively pieces, to be sure, but in a way that lacked both charm and a cantabile manner.

Cantores as used here means church musicians and there is the intriguing reference to the bottles of wine which has been interpreted as a suggestion that Venetian clergy were known to have a fondness for strong drink.

Despite von Uffenbach's reservations about the style of Vivaldi's playing he was deeply impressed by his music, hence his request for *concerti grossi* which were quickly provided, astonishingly quickly to judge from the German's entry in his diary three days later:

Saturday March 9th, 1715.
In the afternoon Vivaldi came to me and brought me, as had been ordered, ten *concerti grossi*, which he said had been composed expressly for me. I bought some of them. In order that I might hear them better he wanted to teach me to play them at once, and on that account he would come to me from time to time. And thus we are to start this very day.

Many observers have questioned the claim by Vivaldi that the *concerti grossi* for von Uffenbach could have been completed in only three days and have dismissed it as a little salesmanship on the part of the composer who had taken them from a stock of such works. It may well be, but it was known that Vivaldi was a highly prolific composer in an age of prolific composers. A composer at this time, especially in Venice, had more in common with the composers of popular chart music today than with the composers of the Romantic period.

Much later in Vivaldi's life, when he was sixty-three, the same

58

brisk approach to composition is recorded by another valuable eye-witness, the Frenchman Charles de Brosses who met him in Venice in 1739. He wrote:

Vivaldi became my intimate friend for the purpose of selling me some very costly concertos. He was partly successful in this and I was successful in what I wanted, which was to hear him and have frequent and good musical diversion. He is a vecchio, who composes furiously and prodigiously. I have heard him undertake to compose a concerto with all its parts more quickly than a copyist could copy it.

Venetian composers were proud of the speed with which they could produce music and Vivaldi, as we have seen, was very much a man of his city. A copy of Vivaldi's opera *Tito Manlio* – one of the operas whose date of performance is not known – claims that it was written *'fatta in 5 giorni'*, that is, in five days. There is evidence of haste in much of Vivaldi's work, especially in the operas, which were sometimes hardly original works but adaptations of former works of his own or of other composers, as was common practice at the time, in an attempt to meet the apparently insatiable public demand for more opera. Examples of Vivaldi's writing betray this great sense of urgency, the notes bending as he writes, as one memorable phrase has it, like 'wheat before the storm'.

The character emerging from these accounts seems to have a well developed sense of business, to show as much of the instincts of the practical man as of the artist. An appreciation of the commercial possibilities of their work was a necessity for composers of the period who were unprotected by legislation. It was a necessity which later composers such as Beethoven and Mozart were to appreciate.

Once a work was published it was regarded as public property and publishing houses simply pirated work for which the composer received nothing. The English publishing house of Walsh & Hare produced pirated versions of Vivaldi's work. Estienne Roger in Amsterdam followed the commercial practice of pirating music published in Italy, so it made sound sense for Vivaldi to deal directly with the Amsterdam publishing firm. There was little consideration of the rights of the composer and copyists were often bribed to pass on works from one publisher to another.

Selling compositions directly to foreign visitors was an ideal solution to the problems of piracy. The composer was able to obtain whatever price the buyer could manage and the buyer had the original compositions to take in triumph to his own country, a point not lost on Vivaldi when assuring Von Uffenbach that the *concerti grossi* had been composed for him alone.

Yet, even given the circumstances of the time, Vivaldi does seem to have had a particular relish for dealing with financial matters, not only in the matter of selling his own compositions but in his work as impresario at the opera houses, an enthusiasm on the part of a priest and a composer which seems strange to modern eyes.

Edward Wright saw him performing in Venice during his travels in Italy 1720-2 and writes:

It is very usual to see priests play in the orchestra. The famous Vivaldi whom they call the Prete Rosso, very well known among us for his concertos, was a topping man among them in Venice.

An even better sighting, with much more information obtained is from the letters of Edward Holdsworth (1684-1746) who visited Italy a number of times, often carrying out buying commissions for Charles Jennens (1700-73) with whom he corresponded. Charles Jennens was a typically cultivated man of the 18th century, a landowner, a lover of music and a man of letters who was a friend of Handel for whom he provided oratorio librettos. He epitomises the period when European people had a common culture, when leisurely travel through the cultural centres of Europe was part of a gentleman's education. Armed with letters of recommendation, a gentleman and his family would be welcomed in the homes and salons of France, Germany and Italy. The privileged shared a common language: French; a common entertainment: music; and a common belief that they were living in the age of enlightenment.

Jennens was a keen admirer of Vivaldi's work and eager to add to his collection, as is clear from a letter by Holdsworth to Jennens:

I had this day some discourse with your friend Vivaldi who told me that he had resolved not to publish any more concertos, because he says it prevents his selling his compositions in MSS which he thinks will turn more to account: as certainly it would if he finds a good market for he expects a guinea for every piece. Perhaps you might deal with him if you were here to choose what you like, but I am sure I shall not venture to choose for you at that price. I had been informed by others that this was Vivaldi's resolution. I suppose you already know he has published 17 concertos.

There is a scandalised note in Holdsworth's reference to the price of a guinea for 'every piece' and his picture of the composer striking a hard bargain about which there can be no compromise is illuminating. Whatever came of these negotiations, Holdsworth continued the search for works by Vivaldi for his friend. He writes from Antwerp in the same year, 1733, with more of his search for the composer's published works:

60

Monsieur Le Cène who has published Vivaldi's and Albinoni's works assured me that if you have 12 of Vivaldi's op and 9 of Albinoni, you have all. Let Vivaldi, he says, reckon as he pleases. He has published no more than 12 and must count several of them double to make up the number 17, which piece of vanity suits very well with his character . . .

Le Cène had taken over the publishing firm of Roger after marrying Roger's eldest daughter, Françoise.

The young Englishman seems to have developed a dislike of the Venetian composer which is hard to understand, certainly at this distance of time, but difficulties were not uncommon in Vivaldi's relationships. He seems to have lacked the knack of establishing easy friendships and Le Cène's impatient remarks that Vivaldi must 'reckon as he please' and the references to his vanity are a typical reaction. Vivaldi may have been vain, of course, but there is no evidence to support the charge and it may be he was accurate in his estimate of the number of concertos published, counting the five sets which are divided into two books, making ten.

Jennens was successful in his efforts to accumulate the works of Vivaldi, in any event. His family bequeathed his collection to the Earl of Aylesford, part of whose musical library was auctioned in 1873, the records of which show all the published works of Vivaldi with the exception of Opus V.

Another contributor to our knowledge of Vivaldi, although not so directly, was the Abbé Conti, who wrote a series of letters to Madame de Caylus from Venice in 1727. These are especially useful as they give evidence of the success Vivaldi enjoyed as an operatic composer and the esteem in which he was held. The Abbé writes on 23 February:

Vivaldi has brought forth three operas in less than three months, two for Venice and the third for Florence; the last has re-established the theatre of that city and brought in much money.

The opera for Florence was *Ipermestra* which was performed at the Teatro della Pergola and the two operas for Venice were *Siroe, re di Persia* and *Orlando furioso*.

In 1727 Vivaldi published his Opus 9, *La cetra* (The Lyre), 11 concertos for violin and one concerto for two violins, which was dedicated to Charles VI (1685-1740) Holy Roman Emperor, a man of wide cultural interests and a composer in his own right. The dedication was evidently appreciated because, as Abbé Conti reports to his correspondent in 1728, the emperor met Vivaldi, probably at Trieste:

The emperor remained for two days at Trieste, but he came neither to

A contemporary painting of Charles VI (1685-1740), Emperor of Austria, King of Bohemia and King of Hungary. He was a patron of the arts and was a gifted musician. In 1728 he met Vivaldi and honoured him with a knighthood. It is thought that Vivaldi may have been hoping for the Emperor's patronage when he made his final visit to Vienna but Charles VI died suddenly in 1740.

Bucari or Fiume. Give my compliments to the count your son; tell him that the emperor gave a large sum of money to Vivaldi along with a chain and a gold medallion and made him a chevalier.

The meeting was successful and much enjoyed by the emperor, as Abbé Conti reports, with a sardonic aside:

The Emperor conversed for a long time with Vivaldi on music; they say that he talked longer to him alone in fifteen days than he talked to his ministers in two years.

This account shows a different Vivaldi to the man haggling over

book on the ground and summoned Mlle Giraud. She came.
'Ah,' he said to her, 'Here is an unusual man, here is an excellent poet. Read this aria. It is this gentleman who has done it here without hedging and in less than quarter of an hour,' and coming back to me, he said: 'Ah, Monsieur, I beg your pardon.' And he embraced me and swore that he would never have another poet but me.
He entrusted me with the drama and ordered the alterations from me. He was always satisfied with me, and the opera succeeded excellently.

The hand of the playwright is evident in this second account, rather more than in the first which is much shorter. In both, the hero of the hour is the poet, but he has a somewhat more bravura role in the second. It is, however, not surprising that the playwright should present himself in the most flattering light, although a strong sense of complacency and self-congratulation is evident, but the essentials are the same: he does go to the composer to arrange the opera, is coldly received by the composer at first because of his youth and because he is unknown to Vivaldi who would prefer to work with a former librettist such as Lalli. In the first version Goldoni makes reference to the singer's ability and there is much less in the way of stage business with breviary and religious observances, but the end is the same: the poet triumphs. Despite its limitations, it is the fullest account we have of Vivaldi as he was and the essentials of the scene show a man of mercurial temperament, suspicious of a young stranger, loyal to a previous collaborator, but quick to praise when pleased.

The inscription on the base of the statue gives an incorrect date for Goldoni, apparently crediting him with the incredible life-span of 1707-1907!

67

More revelations about the nature of this man, Vivaldi, might be expected to be found in paintings of the time. Venice is a city of painters, above everything else, enticing and challenging with its changing light at morning and evening on the swirling waters and the ancient stones of the city. The Accademia Gallery on the Grand Canal houses a brilliant collection of the visions of Venice by the greatest painters of the past. The Bellini brothers, Titian, Tintoretto, Carpaccio; all present a picture of the glittering wonder that was the Most Serene Republic; the grand processions on the Grand Canal or on the Piazzetta San Marco; the richly clothed nobles and priests, the gilded buildings caught in the opalescent light of the Adriatic.

The French Ambassador to Venice in 1495 described his reactions to the city:

They conveyed me along through the great street called the great channel, which is so large that the gallies pass to and fro through it, yea, I have seen hard by the houses ships of four hundred tuns and above. Sure in mine opinion it is the goodliest street in the world and the best built, and reaches in length from the one end of the Towne to the other. Their buildings are high and stately, and all of fine stone. The ancient houses be all painted: but the rest that have been built within these hundred years, have their front all of marble, brought thither out of Istria a hundred miles hence, and are beautiful with many pieces of Porphire and Sarpentine...It is the most triumphant City I ever saw...

A view of Venice by Antonio Canaletto (1697-1768) whose extraordinary paintings of Venice give a precise picture of Venice as it was during the lifetime of Vivaldi.

Contemporary with Vivaldi were painters such as Canaletto, Tiepolo, Longhi and Guardi. Each of them contributes to our understanding of Venice in the 18th century; especially Canaletto who painted the city with extraordinary, almost camera-like fidelity in a series of pictures of calm, masterly assurance. Yet there is

68

nothing of Vivaldi here, no brilliant portrait to add to our knowledge of the man. Again, the biographer has a sense of frustration, imagining what it would have been like to see the composer through the eyes of Goya or Rembrandt.

Some likenesses do exist but they are not especially enlightening. The most interesting and reliable is a sketch in the Vatican Library by Pier Leone Ghezzi drawn when Vivaldi was in Rome in 1722 or 1723. It bears the inscription *Il prete rosso compositore di musica che fece l'opera a Capranica del 1723* (the red priest, composer, who made the opera at Capranica in 1723). It shows a man who does not have the look of a priest; there is nothing of the church about him. He has, if anything, the look of a courtier. The face shown is a type that might be encountered in many paintings, perhaps among the officials of the court, the holder of some minor office, performing small but important services. The face itself is aristocratic, the nose long, the eyes large, the hair long and well cared for. Some observers have claimed to see a pugnacious thrust to the chin or a wilful expression in the eye, but these insights probably owe more to the imagination of the onlooker than the skill of the caricaturist. It is a valuable likeness, however; especially revealing because it does not portray a man of extraordinary, even embarrassing humility, as seen in Vivaldi's dedications, or the capable, even implacable negotiator in the matter of prices for his compositions.

An engraving by the Frenchman François Morellon La Cave made in 1725 gives a much more formal picture than that from Ghezzi. In this the face is much fuller and rounder and the nose less aquiline, although the eyes are large. From the style of the hair it might be that the sitter is wearing a wig. The creative nature of the subject is expressed in the open collar of his shirt and the ribbon that flows from it. There are a number of variations of this engraving which may have been taken from an anonymous painting in the Liceo Musicale of Bologna which was identified as Vivaldi by Francesco Vatielli in 1938 on the grounds that it was similar to the engravings of the composer and that it shows a lock of red hair beneath the wig. If the engravings are of Vivaldi then this painting could also be the composer, but the stiffness of the execution has produced a portrait which gives little idea of the character of the subject, whoever he may have been.

In the 18th century the man of culture would have been equally at home in London, Paris, Vienna and Rome. Travel itself was an essential part of enlightenment and, despite the divisions and differences of Europe, the man of taste would find little to hinder his progress from one country to another. There was at that time a greater unity about what constituted culture than at any period since, certainly among the privileged classes.

69

Musicians followed a similarly peripatetic style since music was the common language of Europe, and the works which were applauded in Amsterdam would be cheered in Dresden. The great composers were great travellers, of necessity; witness the journeyings of Mozart, Haydn and Handel. Vivaldi travelled widely in Italy and beyond, journeys prompted by his increasing fame. From Venice he would be called to the cities of Verona and Florence and Rome and beyond, to Holland, Germany, Austria and Bohemia.

Vivaldi refers to his first period away from Venice in the letter quoted formerly to the Marchese Bentivoglio on 16 November 1739, in which the composer refers to three years of service to the Prince of Darmstadt, Philip of Hesse-Darmstadt, at Mantua. The prince governed Mantua 1707-8 and 1714-35. Music scholars have differed about which three years Vivaldi was in Mantua – Pincherle thought 1720-23 was the likely period; Kolneder suggested 1719-22; later writers such as Talbot and Kennedy feel certain it was 1718-20.

Vivaldi does not appear in the deliberations of the governors of the Pietà from 1718 to 1722 and we know he was in Mantua for much of this period, although he could have returned to Venice often since it was only a short journey.

Mantua became part of the Austrian Empire, under the governorship of the younger brother of the Landgrave of Hesse-Darmstadt, Prince Philip, who took over the city as general of the Imperial army in 1707. The title *Maestro di Cappella di S. A. Il Sig. Principe Filippo Landgravio d'Hassia Darmistath* first appears on the libretto of Vivaldi's opera, *La verità in cimento* in 1720, which was given its first performance in that year at the S. Angelo theatre.

The court of the Gonzagas had been an important musical centre, as we have seen. The musical life of the city did not end with their departure because the governor was clearly not only devout but cultivated. Vivaldi's musical services during his period of service to Philip are not documented, however, but we do know he was deeply involved in the production of operas.

Artabano re de' Parti was produced at the S. Moisè theatre in 1718; *Scanderbeg* at the Teatro della Pergola in Florence in the same year and *Armida al campo d'Egitto* at the S. Moisè, also in the same year. The scale of this activity demonstrates Vivaldi's growing enthusiasm for opera. The librettist of *Artabano re de' Parti* refers to the composer in glowing terms:

A 1725 engraving by La Cave thought to be Vivaldi.

The creative force of. . .which has already commanded all admiration can now claim to your attention to an even greater extent, that you may accord him applause for having enriched the work with new ideas.

71

The incredible baroque façade of the church of San Moisè, near San Marco, which dates from the 8th century. A theatre of the same name was popular during Vivaldi's lifetime but has long since vanished, as have all the theatres which flourished during that period.

The noble names to whom the operas were dedicated reflected the composer's wider stage. *La verità in cimento*, first performed at the S. Angelo in 1720, was dedicated to the privy councillor of His Majesty the Czar and *Armida* to the *Baron Federici Girolamo di Witzendorff signors di Zeger e Seedorff*.

La Candace, o siano Li veri amici was given its first performance at the Teatro Arciducale in 1720 in Mantua. His earlier success for the S. Angelo theatre, *La costanza trionfante,* was performed in Munich in 1718, possibly in the presence of the composer. New works followed in this busy creative period: *Gli inganni per vendetta* at the Teatro delle Grazie, Vicenza, in 1720; *Filippo, re di Macedonia* at the S. Angelo in 1721; *Silvia* at the Nuovo Teatro Ducal in Milan in 1721. On the score of *Tito Manlio* in Turin are the words *Musica del Vivaldi fatta in score 5 giorni* (music by Vivaldi written in five days) which is a bold claim and proof of the pride Venetian composers took in composing at speed.

During Vivaldi's three years in Mantua he was often away attending to the production of his operas in Venice and elsewhere and when his service there ended he continued to be associated with the city – for instance, *Farnace* was performed at the Teatro Arciducale in 1732.

Vivaldi's next great journey, in significance if not in length, was to Rome where we know, according to his own words, he spent three seasons. Two of them are documented – 1723 and 1724 – but the third has not been established. *Ercole sul Termodonte* was first performed at the Teatro Capranica in 1723 and *Giustino* at the same theatre in 1724. It was not uncommon for the clergy to be involved in the operatic life of Rome – the libretto for *Ercole* was by a priest, Don Giacomo Francesco Bussani and *La virtù trionfante dell' amore e dell'odio, ovvero – Il Tigrane* which was presented at the Capranica in 1724 and to which Vivaldi contributed the second act, was by the Abbé Francesco Silvani.

Even for a Venetian, Rome must have been a place to marvel at, and for a priest it was surely the first place in the world, the city of Christ's Vicar on Earth. It was also a major political and cultural centre, a place to which not only the faithful made pilgrimage. Vivaldi was taken up by Roman society; the sketch by Ghezzi referred to earlier is one of a number of such drawings of members of the circle of Cardinal Pietro Ottobini (1667-1740) who came from a noble Venetian family and would have been well aware of the reputation of *Il Prete Rosso*.

His ability as a violinist was widely admired in the Holy City. The two operas he composed for the Rome Carnival seasons provided opportunities for solo violin to display the range of the player's skills which Vivaldi no doubt fully exploited. J. J. Quantz, an earlier admirer of Vivaldi's concertos, arrived in Rome in July 1724, when Vivaldi was in the city. He wrote later of his visit:

I was immediately eager to hear some music; this I could easily manage to do by way of the many churches and monasteries which I visited as much as possible.

The most recent which reached my ears was in the so-called Lombardic style, as yet totally unknown to me, which Vivaldi has introduced to Rome shortly beforehand in one of his operas, and subsequently the local people had taken to it to such an extent that they would hardly listen to anything that was not similar to this style. Meanwhile I at first had great difficulty to find anything pleasing in it and to accustom myself to it; then finally I too found it expedient to conform to the fashion.

Vivaldi did not invent the Lombard rhythm, which Kolneder describes as a slurred figure on the strong beat of the bar, but he made great use of it and was responsible for its popularity. In any event, the Romans loved it and it even reached the ears of the Holy Father himself. Vivaldi wrote of playing for the Pope and being received by him in private apartments on two occasions. We cannot be precise about which Pope it was since Innocent XIII died in March 1724, after a long illness, and was succeeded by Benedict XII in May of that year.

Vivaldi's Roman visit was a professional and social triumph. Applauded as a virtuoso, fêted as a famous composer, admired with a fervour he had never known in his home city.

It is, perhaps, surprising that this distinguished Venetian resumed his contacts with the Pietà in 1723 when there would surely have been many considerable musical posts which would have been open to him, either in Rome or in any number of Italian cities. It is as if Vivaldi could not sever himself completely from the Pietà, perhaps because the musical talents of the pupils excited his musical imagination. The governors of the Pietà were in the familiar position of discussing the question of Don Vivaldi on 2 July 1723, and passed a resolution which recognized the composer's past absences and acknowledged that there would be absences in the future.

The resolution notes: 'In order to maintain the esteem the institution has hitherto gained, it is necessary to make provision for the instrumental concerts, and the administrators of the church and seminary require...every month two of the well-known works of the Rev. Antonio Vivaldi, as he has written two for the present festival of this our own church.' The two works referred to were for the celebration of the Visitation of the Blessed Virgin Mary, and the agreement continued that 'the aforementioned Vivaldi deliver, as he proposes to do, two concertos every month for the time when he is himself in Venice, and during his absence to send these by messenger if this can be done without any especial increase in the cost of transmission.'

A fee of one sequin was to be paid for each work and the governors further stipulated that Vivaldi should direct three or four rehearsals when he was in Venice. The resolution reflects Vivaldi's changed status, as a person of some independence with whom special arrangements must be made, even if unwillingly, and it demonstrates the governors' usual thrifty approach to matters of business in the reference to the cost of any postage of works by Vivaldi being met by the composer and not by the institution.

74

La Fenice, it was built in the final years of the Republic but was destroyed by fire not long after being built. When it was rebuilt in 1836 it was re-created in the sumptuous style of the 18th century and the spectacular stage effects of today echo the lavish spectacles of the theatre in Vivaldi's lifetime.

It is not known how long the contract stood but Kolneder makes the point that if Vivaldi had carried it out to the letter he would have composed some 400 concertos for the Pietà from then until the end of his association with it.

The attempt by the governors to bind Vivaldi more closely to the service of the Pietà was not successful. The demand for him as virtuoso and composer came from many parts of Italy and the rest of Europe. Indeed, the references to him in the painstakingly thorough records of the Pietà grow more scarce in the two years following the agreement and are followed by a complete absence for the years 1723-35. Following his movements in these years is more difficult without the testimony of the Pietà archives but we have the composer's own words about his activities in the previously quoted letter to Bentivoglio of 1737 when he says that 'fourteen years ago we went to a good many European cities'.

His movements in this period are plotted on the evidence of productions of his operas and on occasional direct references to him from contemporary observers such as the Abbé Caylus.

We know he was often in Venice for productions of his own operas: eleven were performed in the city in the period 1725-35, four in 1726. First performances in Venice in 1726 were *Cunegonda*, *La fede tradita e vendicata*; *Farnace*; and *Dorilla in Tempe*. The Abbé Caylus reported on his musical output in a letter of 1727: 'Vivaldi has brought forth three operas in less than three months, two for Venice and the third for Florence.'

Quantz saw him performing during this hectic period: 'Vivaldi had set to music the operas of the S. Angelo theatre and was himself the leader of the orchestra.'

It is likely he was in Venice for the concert of his works performed at the residence of the French Ambassador to Venice to celebrate the birth of twins to the French royal house. The Mercure de France describes the concert at eight in the evening as 'a very beautiful instrumental concert, which lasted nearly two hours, the music for this as well as the Te Deum was by the famous Vivaldi'.

A stay in Naples has been suggested in the period 1727-8 and he was certainly in Florence – the first performance of *Ipermestra* being given at the Teatro della Pergola in 1727 and *L'Atenaide* in 1729. In the libretto to the opera *Adelaide*, performed in Verona in 1735, he is described as 'Don Antonio Vivaldi, maestro di cappella to His Highness the Duke of Lorraine and to His Highness Prince Philip of Hesse-Darmstadt'. The Duke of Lorraine lived in Florence at the time Vivaldi's operas were enjoying huge success there and it is probable the ducal connection was made then.

Vivaldi himself says he went to Vienna, a visit that has been dated in 1728, although not all musicologists agree on the date or even on the visit. The evidence for this visit is based largely on Vivaldi's reference to it and the dedication of the violin concertos, Opus IX, to the Emperor Charles VI in 1728 in which the composer speaks of the 'magnanimous protection' of the Emperor. We have seen from the letters of the Abbé Caylus that the Emperor met and talked to Vivaldi in 1728, probably in Trieste, and was rewarded with money, a gold chain, and a knighthood from the Emperor who was a skilled musician, fond of directing operas from the harpsichord.

Chapter 7

The Four Seasons

The important event of this period was the publication of Vivaldi's Opus VIII, *Il cimento dell'armonia e dell'inventione*, by Michel Le Cène in Amsterdam in 1725. The first four concertos of this opus are *The Four Seasons*, a work which was, and is, extraordinarily popular, demonstrating the vigorous appeal of Vivaldi's musical voice as clearly in this age as when it was heard in the Venice of the 18th century. As with other published works of the time, it was likely that the concertos were already well known and part of the repertoire of the virtuoso-composer.

Il cimento dell'armonia e dell'inventione (The Contest between Harmony and Invention) was a set of 12 concertos for violin dedicated to the 'most illustrious Mr Venceslao, Count of Marzin', a Bohemian nobleman. Vivaldi describes himself as *Maestro in Italia dell'Illustrissimo Conte Sudetto* (Music master to the aforesaid most illustrious Count in Italy). The dedication shows that at least some of the concertos were already known to the Count.

Most Illustrious Sir, when I think of the long succession of years in which I enjoyed the honourable distinction of serving your Highness as maestro di musica in Italy, I blush at the thought that I have not yet given any proof of my profound veneration. Therefore I have decided to have this volume printed in order to lay it most humbly at Your Highness's feet. I beg you not to be surprised if among these few and feeble concertos Your Highness should find *The Four Seasons* which, with your noble bounty, Your Highness has for so long regarded with indulgence. But you may believe that I have found them worthy of appearing in print, because with the sonnets not only are they enhanced by a completely clear interpretation, but so are all the things expressed in them. Therefore I am sure that, although they are the same concertos, they will seem to Your Highness as new.

Vivaldi's humble reference to many years of service to the Count

Ludwig van Beethoven
(1770-1827), a painting by
Isidor Neugasz, 1806.
Beethoven's Pastoral
Symphony is surely a direct
descendant of Vivaldi's The
Four Seasons which was
published in 1725 but had
probably been composed and
performed earlier as is
suggested in the dedication
of the work to Count
Morzin.

is not thought to mean literal service, actually working for the
Count, but supplying music when required.

Le quattro stagioni (The Four Seasons) was immediately popular
throughout Europe, building on the success of *L'estro armonico*
and, in a sense, continuing it.

With *The Four Seasons* Vivaldi moved from the abstract concept
of 18th-century music to what we now know as programme music,
opening up a path which other composers would follow, including
Beethoven whose *Pastoral* is clearly a spiritual descendant of
Vivaldi's magnificent work. There is something patronising

towards programmatic music these days and even an attempt to deny that some works, such as Beethoven's *Pastoral*, are simply descriptive and, indeed, Beethoven instructed players of his symphony 'more expression of feelings than depiction'. There was no such duality in Vivaldi's approach. While he did not invent programme music, he moved it to new levels. His aim was to present the listener with a precise portrayal of the events described in the title or words about the work.

The Four Seasons leaves no doubt about the composer's intentions, not only with the titles of each of the four concertos but with the sonnets which are generally assumed to be the work of Vivaldi himself. It is worth looking at these sonnets because they give a very clear picture of what the music contains.

Spring:
Spring has come, and the birds greet it with happy songs, and at the same time the streams run softly murmuring to the breathing of the gentle breezes. Then, the sky being cloaked in black, thunder and lightning come and have their say. After the storm has quieted, the little birds turn again to their harmonious song.

Each of the concertos is full of vivid descriptions. In *La primavera* (The Spring) the composer is precise in his instructions, saying to the solo violin *il capraro che darme* (the sleeping goatherd) and for the viola *Il cane che grida* (the barking dog). The work is full of felicitous invention: the murmuring of the breeze on three solo violins, the country dancing of the shepherds, the approaching thunderous storm.

L'estate (The Summer) creates the heavy torpor of the Italian summer, the drone of flies, the sound of birds such as the cuckoo and goldfinch (both subjects for future works by Vivaldi).

There is a rich, bawdy flavour in part of *L'autunno* (The Autumn) with drunken shepherds stumbling in attempted dances after too much indulgence. Vivaldi paints a convincing picture, heading one solo section *L'ubriaco* (the drunkard) and beneath it the line *e del liquor*. The solo violin portrays the drunken shepherds in a series of trills and runs until they succumb to drunken slumber in a passage marked *ubriachi dormienti* (sleeping drunks).

L'inverno (The Winter) is brilliant, chillingly creating the world of winter, reminding the listener how cold Venice can be in winter, under the icy blasts from Central Europe sweeping across the Adriatic. This bitter wind, the hesitant steps on frozen ground, the cracking of ice, the comfort of home when the storm rages, are all expressed in eloquent musical language.

The Four Seasons, because of its explicit nature, says much about the composer who is expressing his own ideas about the world around him. It is the work of a man of some humanity, acutely aware of the physical world and of the manners of men: consider, for example, the humorous observation of the drunken shepherds. In this music we do not see the calculating businessman depicted by Holdsworth or the embarrassingly humble servant of the dedications. This is a wise, mature and sensitive description of the year. The rustic melodies of the Veneto are echoed in parts of the work, evidence of an awareness of the natural world about him by Vivaldi who, like many other composers, is influenced by the sounds of nature.

Le quattro stagioni's pictorial purpose is in keeping with the 18th century's feelings about the significance of the 'natural world'; that world to which poets and painters, as well as musicians, addressed themselves. Charles Henri Blainville spoke for his time in his *Esprit de l'art musical* in 1754:

Franz Joseph Haydn (1732-1809) whose enormous output of music includes descriptive music—for example, The Seasons—which clearly owes a debt to Vivaldi's The Four Seasons.

Vivaldi's music was popular in France, especially the Four Seasons, which was a particular favourite of Louis XV who was entertained by a concert of La Primavera performed by nobles of the court in 1730.

Study nature. You see what variety and contrasts it offers to you. There it is, an arid desert bounded by steep crags, the abode of silence and dread. Here is a pleasant plain of tufted slopes and a verdant meadow bedecked with flowers where everything breathes gaiety.

Or else you depict the effects of storm or tempest – subterranean sound, the whistling of the winds, the heaving of the waves of the sea, the noise of the waters mingling with the noise of thunder; let everything portray the confusion and havoc that this short-lived strife causes. But the sun re-appears, the wind drops, the air becomes quiet and serene, the birds revert to proclaiming by their sweet twitterings the peace of the elements.

81

Jacques Lacombe was in complete agreement in his *Le Spectacle de Beaux-Arts* of 1758:

The spectacle that the fine arts present to us is none other than that of beautiful nature. The visual arts convey it to the eye, music to the ear, poetry to the imagination. It is always nature that is perceived in their pleasing products.

The work enjoyed particular popularity in France where the school of natural philosophy flourished. The Concert Spirituel performed *The Four Seasons* in Paris in 1728, according to the *Mercure de France*, which noted: 'Next, Vivaldi's concerto of *The Four Seasons*, which is an excellent symphonic piece, was played.'

La primavera became the favourite of the four concertos, enjoying royal favour, again according to the *Mercure de France* of December 1730:

The king asked next that Vivaldi's Primavera, which is an excellent symphonic piece, be played, and as the musicians of the king were not as a rule at this concert, the prince de Dombes, the count d'Eu and several other lords of the court were willing to accompany Monsieur Guignon so as not to deprive His Majesty of hearing this beautiful symphonic piece, which was performed to perfection.

The concerto received a number of treatments; Jean Jacques Rousseau arranged it for solo flute in 1755 and a Nicholas Chedville in 1793 asked for a licence to publish *La primavera* and other Italian works 'to adapt, to transpose and to arrange in a way easy to be performed on the musette, the hurdy-gurdy, or the flute with the accompaniment of violins and a bass'. The enthusiasm of the French for the work was almost boundless and *La primavera* was arranged as a motet, *Laudate Dominum de Coelis*, by Michel Corette in 1765 with the subtitle *Motet a Grand Choeur arrange dans le Concerto de Printemps de Vivaldi*.

Many of Vivaldi's works have titles which are descriptive. Some, like *L'estro armonico* indicate an idea or theory; others like *The Cuckoo* or *The Goldfinch* introduce the sound of the bird named in the title; some, such as *L'inquietudine* (unrest) or *Il reposo* (repose), are atmospheric. Storm music was especially popular in the 18th century, an indispensable part of any opera, and so were bird effects such as those in *The Goldfinch* and *The Cuckoo* concertos. The latter was very popular in England but some found it wearying after a number of hearings, as Doctor Burney writes:

His Cuckoo Concerto, during my youth, was the wonder and delight of all frequenters of country concerts; and Woodcock, one of the Hereford waits, was sent for far and wide to perform it. If acute and rapid tones are evils, Vivaldi has much of the sin to answer for.

Some twenty-eight of Vivaldi's works have descriptive titles. Some were probably bestowed on the works by others, and others give examples of a sense of humour at work which is probably Vivaldi's. *Il proteo ossia il mondo al rovescio* (Proteus, or the World Upturned) is a concerto for violin, cello, orchestra and basso continuo in which the solo violin part is given in the tenor and bass clefs and the cello part in the treble clef with the direction: 'The solo violin can play the solos of the cello and conversely the cello those of the violin.' There is also a distinctly playful element in Vivaldi's dedication to Pisendel for concerto RV574 which has the initials P.S.A.S.I.S.P.G.M.D.G.S.M.B. which has been translated as: 'For His Serene Highness the Signor Pisendal Giorgio'.

The Gazette d'Amsterdam advertised the forthcoming appearance of Vivaldi's Opus IX in January 1729; and *La cetra* (The Lyre), eleven concertos for violin and one for two violins was published in November of that year. The work, as we have seen, was dedicated to Charles VI, the Austrian Emperor, who later rewarded the composer handsomely. There is some doubt about the composer's movements in the period 1729-31. There is nothing in the records of the Pietà about him and there is no evidence of his usual operatic activity. Some observers think he may have been ill because, by his own admission, he was a sick man and was now approaching the age of fifty and had had an unusually hectic life.

Vital information was discovered by Rodolfo Gallo in the Venetian archives in 1938 which concerned a matter considered by the authorities in September 1729. On 30 September, Giovanni Battista Vivaldi, the father of the composer, asked for permission to leave the services of the ducal chapel for one year so he could accompany his son to Germany. The son is not named but it is safe to assume it was Antonio, rather than one of his brothers. Vivaldi's standing at the court of Charles VI, at Vienna, would have made a stay in that city an eminently sensible idea. It is possible he visited Darmstadt since he still carried the title of *maestro di cappella* to Philip, Lundgrave of Hesse-Darmstadt and there would have beeen every reason for visiting Dresden, where his friend and admired pupil, G. Pisendel, was the soloist in the royal orchestra.

Dealings with Le Cène may have taken him to Amsterdam and it may be that the third, unaccounted, season of Roman opera took place in this period.

Modern scholars suggest he was active in Bohemia during the period, although the evidence is only circumstantial. His opera

L'Argippo was performed in Prague in the autumn of 1730 and *Farnace* had been well received in the city in the spring of that year.

Vivaldi's opera *La costanza trionfante degl' amori e degl' odi*, first performed in 1716, was staged at the S. Angelo theatre in 1731 in a new arrangement and with a new title, *L'Odio vinto dalla costanza*. The work was arranged by A. Galeazzi, an obscure composer, which is a little surprising because Vivaldi was not a man to allow others to tinker with his music. The fact that such a thing happened at all has led to the conclusion that Vivaldi was either ill or absent from Venice at the time. In the same year, his *Armida al campo d'Egitto* was given at the Teatro Santa Margherita, but in this production Vivaldi's original score was abandoned and the music provided by several composers. Again, it was a situation Vivaldi would have been unlikely to approve had he been present. It is also possible that there was some disenchantment with Vivaldi's operatic works, the first shadow on his musical popularity, or it may have been connected with a new impresario at the S. Angelo Theatre which had been returned to its legal owners, Bernardo Cappello and Benedetto Marcello.

This Benedetto Marcello (1686-1739) is an important figure, for himself and for his part in Vivaldi's story. He was also a gifted composer, like Vivaldi, and came from a noble family, unlike Vivaldi. It is possible that the two men knew each other, or were certainly aware of each other. Marcello was a pupil of Lotti and Gasparini and his major musical output is concerned with religious themes. His most important compositions were his settings of fifty psalms. As a nobleman, he did not compose for money and served the state in a number of posts, accepting the duties of a Venetian patrician.

Marcello's musical standing is high in Italy and beyond, but he is also significant as a writer, especially as a satirist, in the work *Il Teatro alla moda* (The Theatre in Fashion). This is a biting comment on the musical world of the time and scores a number of palpable hits, although it was not realised that Vivaldi was a principal target until a discovery made by Francesco Malipiero in 1930 which established the date of the work and discovered at whom it was aimed. The title page shows an unusual collection of characters, rather like something out of Lewis Carroll, in a boat rowed by a gondolier but with two oars; at the stern, steering the vessel is a small angel playing a violin and wearing a priest's hat, while at the bow is a bear carrying a flag on his shoulder. The boat carries provisions, notably a large cask of wine.

Malipiero's discovery of an annotated version of *Il Teatro alla moda* identified these figures. The angel in the priest's hat sawing away at the violin represents Vivaldi and the S. Angelo theatre for which he provided so many operas. The gondolier is Modotto,

Il Teatro Alla Moda, published anonymously in 1720, was a witty attack on a number of practices and personalities in the world of Venetian music, including Vivaldi who is vigorously lampooned. The author was Benedetto Marcello (1686-1739), a patrician and composer. There is no evidence that he and Vivaldi met but they clearly knew of each other and Marcello was a pupil of Gasparini's.

IL
TEATRO
ALLA MODA
O SIA
METODO sicuro, e facile per ben comporre, & efequire l'OPERE Italiane in Musica all'uso moderno,

Nel quale

Si danno Avvertimenti utili, e necessarij à Poeti, Compositori di Musica, Musici dell'uno, e dell'altro sesso, Imprefarj, Suonatori, Ingegneri, e Pittori di Scene, Parti buffe, Sarti, Paggi, Comparfe, Suggeritori, Copisti, Protettori, e MADRI di Virtuofe, & altre Persone appartenenti al Teatro.

DEDICATO

DALL' AUTTORE DEL LIBRO AL COMPOSITORE DI ESSO.

Stampato ne BORGHI di BELISANIA per ALDIVIVA LICANTE, all'Insegna dell'ORSO in PEATA. Si vende nella STRADA del CORALLO alla PORTA del PALAZZO d'ORLANDO.

E si ristamperà ogn'anno con nuova aggiunta.

the impresario of the S. Angelo theatre, who once had a boat business, and the bear is a punning reference to Orsatto who was the impresario of the S. Moisè theatre. The flag carried by the bear appeared on the tickets of the S. Moisè theatre. The booklet carried the information that it was 'printed in the suburbs of Belisania Aldiviva Licante at the sign of the Bear in the Boat. For sale in Coral Street at the gate of Orlando's Palace'.

Aldiviva is identified as *Aldiviva: Mon. Vivaldi, virtuoso celebre di violino e compositore delle opere in Sant'Angelo* (Aldiviva: Vivaldi, the celebrated violin virtuoso and composer of operas at the Sant'Angelo). Anagrams of this kind were often used in pamphlets of the period – Licante was Canteli, a female singer at the S. Moisè theatre; Borghi di Belisania represented Borghi and Belisani, two male singers at the S. Angelo theatre, and so on.

The title page announced that the book was 'a sure and easy method for composing Italian operas well, and for performing them in the modern manner. Containing useful and necessary directions for poets, composers, singers of both sexes, impresarios, buffa parts, tailors, pages, supers, prompters, copyists, patrons and mothers of female singers and others belonging to the theatre'.

The annotated version describes Vivaldi's part in the entertainment:

Through the angel in the shape of the protector or guardian of the boat we are given to understand the theatre of which the aforesaid Signor Modotto is the impresario, but through the hat on its head and the violin held by the angel, who has its foot in the air, it comes to signify Vivaldi, in whom the aforesaid Modotto puts his entire trust.

The author of the satire clearly has great fun in mocking a whole range of personalities in Venetian operas and takes, perhaps, a special pleasure in dealing with Vivaldi.

It will be no bad thing that the composer has been for many years a violinist or viola player, and even a copyist for some famous composer, whose originals he has kept.
Before composing the opera, the composer is advised to consult all the principal singers and arrange to provide them with arias tailored to their talents. These arias should be alternately merry or grave, regardless of the words, and it is emphasised that the best arias must go to the prima donnas.

Marcello attacks the excesses of the Venetian opera, which clearly he knew well, probably from the singer, Rosanne Scalfi, whom he later married.

Singers do not escape his mockery, however, especially the popular *castrati*. In his advice to such singers, Marcello advises:

If he is on stage with another character, who addresses him in play, or sings an aria, he will greet the masks in the boxes, smile at the musicians, the extras, etc., so that the public will understand quite clearly that it is he, Signor Alipio Fornconi, and not Prince Zoroaster that he is supposed to be representing.

These squibs must have delighted Venetian readers since Marcello describes to perfection how the singers actually behaved. The would-be composer is advised the treat the singers, particularly the *castrati*, with deep respect and to walk with hat in hand, one pace to the rear of them, as an indication of this respect.

There are nicely aimed shots at Vivaldi. A comment on the manner of dedicating the work suggests the deepest humility in approach, with full use of expressions such as freedom and magnanimity, and might close with the composer kissing the flea bites of His Excellency's dog as a signal of his profound humility.

The arrow found its target perfectly, recalling Vivald's obeisance when dedicating his works. His dedication to Count Morzin speaks of 'blushing' at the thought of not having given proof of his 'profound veneration' but an even more striking example is the dedication of Opus II in which the composer sinks into an attitude of even deeper humility: 'You have descended from your throne, and this condescension has permitted Your Highness to console him who, deeply obeisant, confesses himself unworthy to kiss even the lowest step of your throne.'

The librettist is not forgotten. It said it is better he knows nothing of metre or versification. He need know nothing of the work of ancient poets but can allude to such figures as Horace and Aristotle in his foreword. A principal concern should be to consult with the manager on the number of changes of scene required and the kind of stage machinery to be employed for effects. After this, it is necessary to talk to scene shifters who will tell him about the length of time which should be given to arias and recitatives to

Benedetto Marcello (1686-1739), author of Il Teatro Alla Moda (The Theatre in Fashion) and a gifted composer.

allow time for the preparation of the set. The recitatives, he is reminded, need have no connection with anything taking place on the stage, but should be long enough for the opening to be forgotten by the time the middle has been reached.

Marcello warns the composer how to react if the impresario is not immediately transported by the music. Tell him, he says, that the score contains many more notes than usual, up to a third more, and that it took almost fifty hours to compose.

The impresario's responsibilities are also described. The first thing is that he should have no knowledge of the theatre and should follow certain rules when commissioning an opera – for example, if the work is to be staged on the twelfth of the month, there will be time enough for the composer to complete the work if he is commissioned on the fourth. He should make sure that everything in the opera ends happily and that the music is so organised that all the prinicipal singers receive equal treatment; if two prima donnas appear they should have the same number of arias and, to be completely fair, the same number of syllables.

There is no evidence of Vivaldi and Marcello meeting but it must be beyond doubt that they knew each other. Benedetto Marcello was a pupil of Vivaldi's former superior at the Pietà, Gasparini. There were also matters arising from the lease of the land on which the S. Angelo theatre stood. The lease was the subject of much disagreement with the legal owners, of whom Marcello was one, fighting a long battle to have it restored to them. Vivaldi's father was cited in legal documents as a debtor in 1714 and Vivaldi acted as impresario and conductor at the theatre on many occasions until it was restored to the Marcello and Cappello families in 1737.

There were grounds enough for a grudge against *Il Prete Rosso* on this matter alone. Furthermore, Benedetto Marcello was a patrician and Antonio Vivaldi a commoner. The ironic condescension with which Marcello regarded Vivaldi suggests that he saw him as a musical parvenu and it may have been an opinion shared by others, perhaps by some of the governors of the Pietà.

Benedetto Marcello was educated, a patrician, devoted to music as a cultural and religious expression rather than as a means of winning fame and fortune. Vivaldi was the son of a barber-violinist, an exaggerated, colourful figure, a public man with his dazzling virtuosity as a violinist, a prolific composer of popular music for the opera, vigorously involved in increasing his fortunes through music. For some, Marcello is still the authentic voice of Venetian music. His name is honoured in the Venetian conservatory near the campo San Stefano and his music is revered. Vivaldi, one feels, has been honoured lately, perhaps even reluctantly in his native city, after being virtually wiped from its consciousness.

Opera was Vivaldi's major activity in the period before and

Verona, the theatre—this city saw the first performances of a number of Vivaldi's operas including *Adelaide*, which many consider to be his finest operatic work.

during the supposed journey to Bohemia, but his instrumental compositions continued. Opus X, published in 1728 by Le Cène in Amsterdam, was six concertos for flute.

Vivaldi wrote many works for flute and recorder, probably for pupils at the Pietà who were especially talented on these instruments and for a virtuoso such as Quantz whom he met in Venice in 1726. The lower-pitched recorder which had been widely used in chamber music was being superseded by the flute which was more penetrating and more versatile. Vivaldi wrote extensively for both instrument, using the term *flauto* for the recorder and *flauto traverso* for the transverse flute. Five concertos for violin and one for oboe made up Opus XI which appeared in 1729 and Opus XII, five concertos for violin and one without a solo instrument, appeared in the same year.

By 1731 or 1732 the composer had probably returned to Italy. A new opera, *Semiramide* was performed in Verona in 1731 and repeated at Mantua the next year. The first performance of another new opera, *La fida ninfa*, which had a libretto by a Venetian nobleman, Scipione Maffei, took place at the Teatro Filarmonico in Verona in 1732. With such great musical events taking place, and knowing Vivaldi's involvement in the production of his operas, it is likely that the composer was present and active in these productions.

89

Pietro Metastasio
(1698-1782), poet and
librettist. He provides the
texts for a number of
Vivaldi's operas, including
L'Olimpiade, which was
given its first performance at
the S. Angelo in Venice in
1734.

Vivaldi was in Venice in 1733 when Edward Holdsworth had unsatisfactory negotiations in the matter of buying original works. In that same year Vivaldi returned to the S. Angelo theatre with a new opera, *Montezuma*. Another opera, *Sarce*, is given in Kolneder's list of Vivaldi's operas as having its first performance in 1733.

One of his finest operas, *L'Olimpiade*, with a libretto by Metastasio, was performed at the S. Angelo theatre in 1734. It was this opera which was chosen for the first modern performance of an opera by Vivaldi in Siena in 1939. It is a work of great richness, the quality of which was described by the pioneering producers:

The choice of L'Olimpiade from the numerous Vivaldi operas which can be found in the National Library in Turin was influenced above all by consideration of the extremely beautiful libretto by Metastasio; but also on account of the unusual beauty of the music.

However, despite their admiration of the libretto and music, drastic cuts and alterations were needed to reduce the length of the recitatives, and music was taken from another Vivaldi opera, *Dorilla in Tempe*, to replace passages which had been lost from the original.

Chapter 8

Anna Girò

During the outpouring of operas, Vivaldi again appears at the Pietà. It is impossible to say what drew him there after an absence of ten years during which he was a celebrated visiting virtuoso and composer, busily engaged in the production of operas and concerts. His output was considerable; six operas between 1731 and 1734, at Venice, Verona and Ancona. These operas appear to have been successful, which would mean the composer was also a man of considerable financial means. Yet he reappears in the deliberations of the governors of the Pietà in 1735 and is reappointed *maestro de' concerti* at an annual salary of 100 ducats. He is again very much in the position of employee, important for the musical education of the Pietà, but by no means an ideal choice. There is a marked change of tone in the account when it is compared to that before Vivaldi's prolonged absence when the governors were obliged to recognise Vivaldi's status as a composer and were forced to treat him with respect. All that had changed; the tone of the governors was brisk, peremptory even. He was to supply music for all manner of instruments and was reminded that he had to be present with *dovuta frequenza*. The independence of the impresario, composer and virtuoso seems a thing of the past as the governors comment *'senza idea di piu partire come aveva praticato negli anni passati'* (without a view of leaving ever again as has been his custom in the past).

But the renewal of his appointment at the Pietà made no difference at all to his operatic output which, if anything, increased. The aim of the governors in having Vivaldi at the exclusive service of the Pietà was clearly a failure.

The year 1735, when Vivaldi was fifty-seven, was a momentous one for the composer. It marked his return to the musical world of the Pietà (to obtain a position for his later declining years; drawn by musical possibilities of the gifted and ardent young pupils or the serenity of the establishment, a contrast to the competitive and

The Pietà where Vivaldi had at his disposal an enthusiastic and gifted army of musicians and which he made famous as one of the outstanding musical establishments of Venice.

tempestuous operatic scene?).

It was in this year that he met Carlo Goldoni, who was then twenty-eight, the coming man of the theatre whose *Il Belisario* had been put on at the S. Samuele theatre in 1734 and was a great success. Carlo Goldoni (1707-1793), a Venetian, was to become famous for his comedies but was then establishing himself as a librettist and was eager to work with the famous Vivaldi, as he admits in his memoirs. He provides the most important firsthand information we have about Vivaldi in this period and, indeed, our view of the man and his character is based almost entirely on Goldoni's impressions. The fleeting glimpses of the previous ten years are replaced by an authentic contemporary account, as we have seen earlier in the quotation from Goldoni's *Mémoires* published in French in 1787, a second and fuller version of his memories of meeting *Il Prete Rosso* for the first time.

The younger man had some reservations about the musical abilities of the priest, however, as he revealed in the first account of their meeting:

That year, for the Ascension opera, the composer was the priest, Vivaldi, known as the red priest because of his hair, and sometimes referred to as Rossi, so that people thought that was his surname.

This most famous violinist, this man famous for his sonatas, especially for those known as the Four Seasons, also composed operas; and although the really knowledgeable people say that he was weak on counterpoint and that he handled his basses badly, he made the parts sound well, and most of the time his operas were successful.

While Goldoni's rather dismissive attitude towards the older man's compositions may have been a gifted and ambitious young man's attitude towards an established figure, it confirms that Vivaldi was more highly regarded as a violinist than as a composer by many of his contemporaries.

The collaboration was successful and the opera discussed in his *Mémoires*, *Griselda*, was performed at the S. Samuele theatre in Venice in 1735. The opera concerns the adventures of a shepherdess, Griselda, in Thessaly. The opera itself is typical of its time with very long recitatives – nine pages of score at the beginning – but with some fine arias. The principal role is taken, as the libretto informs us, by 'La Signora Anna Girò'. This lady plays a crucial role in Vivaldi's story, as the composer himself said in his correspondence with Bentivoglio. It is to Carlo Goldoni that we owe most of our knowledge of her, as we do of Vivaldi.

In his account of the negotiations about the opera *Griselda* Goldoni writes:

That year the role of the prima donna was to be taken by Signora Annina Girò (or Giraud), the daughter of a wigmaker of French origin, who was commonly called Annina of the red priest, because she was Vivaldi's pupil. She did not have a beautiful voice, nor was she a great musician, but she was pretty and attractive; she acted well.

The relationship between Vivaldi and Anna Girò was a long one and well known to Venice. It is thought he met her while he was in the service of the 'God fearing' Prince Philip of Hesse-Darmstadt in 1718-20. Anna Girò – sometimes her name is given in the French style of Giraud rather than the Italian form – may have been born in Mantua because she was sometimes described as 'Mantovana'; people were often identified in this way at the time. There has been speculation that Anna might have been a pupil at the Pietà, based in part on Vivaldi's claim that she was his pupil, and there is a girl of the same Christian name in the list of those performing *Moyses Deus Pharaonis* in 1714 but Goldoni's account of her parentage is more reliable. If she had been associated with the Pietà he would have known of it and surely added it to his vivid sketch of her.

There were whispers about the nature of the relationship between the singer and the composer and, later on, rather more than whispers. The world of opera was part of the fashionable scene, the players were all too human, many of the singers were available for other duties at a price, according to contemporary sources.

Venice at this time was at its most frenetic, a whirligig of pleasure. All desires could be gratified in this most worldly of cities. The bordellos of Venice were famous throughout Europe; her courtesans (more than 11,000 catalogued at the end of the 16th century) were beautiful and sought after. Sensuality hung in the air, like a faintly scented cloud over the city. Music throbbed across the dappled water of the lagoon as gondolas carried amorous passengers to secret parts of the darkness, their discreet, grave, forms prompting Byron's lines that they 'contain a deal of fun, like mourning coaches when the funeral's done'.

Visitors from Northern Europe, like Byron, were drawn to the city of the sea, escaping from the restrictions of their society, attracted by the exotic life of Venice. The Victorians loved the city, thrilling to its wicked past. John Ruskin, author of that monumental work, *The Stones of Venice*, was keenly aware of the sordid aspects of the city's history which furnished many examples for philosophical speculations and splendid prose as in:

The point I wish to impress upon the reader is, that the bright hues of the early architecture of Venice were no sign of gaiety of heart, and that the investiture with the mantle of colours by which she is known by all other cities of Italy and Europe, was not granted to her in the fever of festivity but in the solemnity of early and earnest religion. She became in after times the revel of the earth, the masque of Italy; and therefore she is now desolate: but her glorious robe of gold and purple was given to her when first she rose a vestal from the sea, not when she became drunk with the wine of her fornication.

Vivaldi, as we know, did not follow the duties of a priest. He was a man of musical affairs, an impresario, a virtuoso, a composer. In a city such as Venice, in the society of opera, it is easy to see why the relationship between Vivaldi and Anna Girò would be assumed to be more than simply musical.

The convents of the city were not known for piety. The nuns of S. Lorenzo were notorious for their casual behaviour which drew fascinated and censorious comments from foreign visitors. Edward Wright gives a convincing description of the life of the convent when he writes:

On their feast days the door of their convent is flung open, and they stand in crowds at the entrance, where I observed them talking to their acquaintance with great freedom. Nor do these noble vestals at any time confine themselves to such close restrictions as others of their order are obliged to do. Those I saw at Celestia were dressed in white; no veil over their faces; a small transparent black covering goes round their

Opposite:
The worldly atmosphere of the convents is captured in this painting by Pietro Longhi in the 18th century.

94

95

shoulders; their heads were very prettily dressed; a sort of small thin coif went round the crown, and came under the chin; their hair was seen at the forehead, and nape of the neck; the covering on their neck and breast was so thin, that t'was next to nothing at all.

A charming picture, although it should be remembered that some of the nuns were not in the convents of their own choice but had been placed there by their noble families.

Charles de Brosses was enthusiastic about the nuns he saw in Venice in 1738 and happily passed on the latest gossip about them.

There is a furious dispute amongst the three convents of the city to decide which will have the advantage of giving a mistress to the new nuncio who has just arrived. In truth, it would be towards the nuns that I would turn most willingly if I had to stay here for long. All those that I have seen at Mass, through the grille, talking the whole of the time and laughing together, have seemed pretty to me and got up in such a way to set off their beauty. They have a charming little hairstyle, a simple habit but, of course, almost entirely white, which uncovers their shoulders and throat no more and no less than the Roman costumes of our actresses.

Anna Girò had a musical career of her own, independent of Vivaldi, which rather undermines the theory that she was merely his mistress. Her first operatic appearance in Venice was in 1724 in the opera *Laodicea* by Albinoni and she was engaged for operas by other leading composers of the day such as Hasse and Galuppi, all of which suggests that Goldoni's opinion of her singing ability may not have been universal.

Anna Girò made her first appearance in an opera by Vivaldi in 1726. The opera was the highly successful *Farnace* which was presented at the S. Angelo theatre and marked the beginning of a long operatic association in which, as Vivaldi himself said, she became indispensable to his music.

The Abbé Conti saw the opera and passed his judgement of it to his correspondent, Madame de Caylus:

The libretto is passable if you ignore the faults of an episode in it contrary to all possibilities. The music is by Vivaldi. It is very varied in the sublime and tender; his pupil does wonders in it, although her voice is not of the most beautiful.

The Abbé evidently shared Goldoni's opinion of her singing ability, but Vivaldi had no reservations about it because she sang principal roles in his operas in Venice and throughout their travels

96

which Vivaldi referred to in a letter of 1737: 'Fourteen years ago we went together to a good many European cities.'

Vivaldi was constant in his denials about any impropriety in their relationship, pointing out that they were always accompanied by a retinue of others, necessary because of his ill health, including her sister, Paolina, who acted as his nurse. Vivaldi commented on the burden of the expense this put him to and there is some evidence that the sisters were part of his household, with others, but the composer later denied that this was so.

These matters came to the forefront of Vivaldi's affairs in the period 1737-9 when his personal life assumed a greater importance than was usual or welcome at a time he was engaged in busy musical activity for the theatre and for the Pietà. Much light is thrown on these years – although there are also, alas, many dark corners – from information in the surviving correspondence with

A fete day in Venice by Antonio Canaletto, the kind of scene which Vivaldi would have known.

A stunning painting entitled The Mandolin by Giovanni Tiepolo (1692-1769). The mandolin enjoyed considerable popularity in the 18th century and Vivaldi composed for the instrument, probably for his patron, the Marchese Bentivoglio d'Aragona.

the Marchese Guido Bentivoglio d'Aragona, which we have quoted earlier.

Bentivoglio was born in Venice in 1705 and went to Rome as a young man, probably to take up a career in the church, but was obliged to leave Rome when his elder brother died and return to the family estates at Ferrara to become the head of the family.

From the surviving letters between the Marchese and Vivaldi, it appears they met in Rome but the year of the meeting is not known. 1723 or 1724 are the most likely years although it may have been during the third, undated, visit by Vivaldi to the Roman opera season. Again, from the correspondence it appears the nobleman knew the Girò sisters. From the tone of Vivaldi's letters, it seems likely that he had not met Bentivoglio for some time. At one point he asks if the nobleman still plays the mandolin and receives the rather cool reply that he picks up the instrument once a year or less. The reference to the mandolin has led to speculation that Vivaldi's compositions for mandolin were for this particular player, which is possible, but they might have also been written for pupils of the Pietà or for general consumption since the mandolin was a highly popular instrument at the time. The theme of the letters is Vivaldi's attempts to set up an opera season in Ferrara, attempts which were dogged by ill fortune.

At first, all went well. Bentivoglio was receptive to the idea and sent the Abbé Bollani, impresario of the Ferrara opera, to Venice to discuss the plan. The meeting was successful, as Vivaldi wrote on 3 November 1736, with enthusiasm about the quality of the company:

I assure Your Excellency that we have succeeded in bringing together such a company as, I hope, will not have been seen on the stage at Ferrara for many years.

Vivaldi adds that he is busily engaged at the S. Cassiano theatre in Venice and complains that he has turned down an invitation to write the third opera of the theatre's season because they offered 90 sequins instead of his usual fee of 100. Having established his usual scale of fees, Vivaldi goes on:

However, Ferrara will have two operas that will seem to have been composed specially, since they will be entirely adapted and revised in my hand for only six sequins each, which is the fee of a copyist.

The suggestion here is of unusual generosity on the part of Vivaldi in providing two operas, admittedly re-worked, for the cost of a copyist's fee.

The period of harmony was short. Soon Vivaldi formed a deep mistrust of Bentivoglio's emissaries, especially the Abbé Bollani. In a letter of 29 December 1736 Vivaldi explodes with indignation:

Having just returned from Ferrara he pestered me to turn out Ginevra immediately. Forthwith I adapted the original and had the parts copied, which I sent to Your Excellency as a token; the parts for Moro and the tenor, however, are still in their hands.
Scarcely had this been done than a new order came: these gentlemen no longer wanted Ginevra but Demetrio. I go to look for it at the Grimani palace in order to have it copied, but I see that out of six parts, five must be changed; hence it follows that the recitatives come out all wrong. I therefore decided (Your Excellency can form an opinion of my good will from this) to do over all the recitatives. I ought to inform Your Excellency that in addition to the six sequins, I concluded an agreement with the aforementioned impresario that he would pay for all the copies of the

vocal and instrumental parts. Thus, when Demetrio is completely put into shape again, I have the vocal and instrumental parts copied, I have all the singers learn their rôles by heart, I hold three rehearsals, and I get everything set. I am sure that such delight has not been got from the opera before.

All this being done, I tell him that between Ginevra and Demetrio I have spenty fifty lire for the vocal and instrumental parts. And although one opera alone cost him thirty lire, there are a good ten letters in which I entreat him to give orders to this Lanzetti for the payment of the other twenty, and he has never answered me on that score. Through a number of messengers he pestered me to send him *L'Olimpiade*. I arrange or, rather, spoil my original manuscript by patching it up. I have some passages copied under my very eyes, still without having received the order for it, because I believe it is in his interest by reason of the difference there is between one copyist and another. And then comes a new order; they no longer want *L'Olimpiade* but *Alessandro nell'Indie*...

Much of Vivaldi's part in this correspondence is about money he has paid out and which he has not yet received, and it has to be said that the injured tone adopted by the composer is not attractive and it may be that Bentivoglio found it trying. We know from other accounts that Vivaldi was a keen bargainer. Holdsworth and de Brosses provide evidence on this account although it should be remembered that a man in Vivaldi's position had to look after his own interests. Published music was not protected by legislation and the sale of manuscripts privately was the best way of protecting compositions and obtaining the maximum price for them.

Vivaldi was displaying a national trait in his financial dealings, for the Venetians had a reputation for skilled and ruthless trading. In its great days the city state traded with Jews and Christians and Muslims without distinction, pursuing profit with single-minded zeal.

Some observers suspect less than total honesty on Vivaldi's part in these dealings, particularly in exaggerating the extent of the expenses he incurred, but the negotiations are so tortuous and there are such gaps in the correspondence that it is difficult to be certain, and to make a judgement would be unfair.

There is, perhaps, something obsessive in Vivaldi's anxiety about money. On 2 January 1739, Vivaldi wrote to the Marchese with the third act of *Alessandro*, with a special plea:

I implore Your Excellency to exert his authority so that the impresario put immediately into the hand of Signora Girò the six sequins and twenty lire for copying that I ought to have in all justice. I hear the opera is too long and it was certain that an opera of four hours was not suitable for Ferrara.

A glimpse of life in the early part of the 18th century through eyes of Pietro Longhi: a young girl hears what adventures the future has in store.

Vivaldi confessed that things were not going well at the S. Cassiano theatre for which he had refused to compose another opera because it was so badly run and the tickets cost so much it was impossible to cover the costs.

The negotiations for the Ferrara season of opera displeased everyone. At the end of the season there is a distinctly chilly note in a letter from Bentivoglio which is in response to a letter from Vivaldi thanking the nobleman for the help he had given to Vivaldi and the Girò sisters.

I have done little, or nothing, for the Girò ladies. I certainly had – and still have – the desire to do something more than the clearly manifested consideration that I have for their quality. Nonetheless, you ought not to thank me for this very slight inclination that I have given them here. As for your visit to these parts, I will be happy to see you, but do not put yourself out in any way.

The last lines suggest the Marchese had no enthusiasm for a meeting but it seems Vivaldi was not unduly offended, because, unabashed, he returned to his patron in a letter dated 3 May 1737, describing the success of his latest opera, *Catone in Utica*, which was given its première in Verona, from where Vivaldi wrote. After only six performances the opera had covered its cost and there was every prospect of a handsome profit. Vivaldi was full of confidence once more and the carping about money matters had quite vanished. He wrote as a successful impresario and composer:

101

A similar opera, composed in part to another text, I would think able to command a comparable sum also in Ferrara. However, it is not suitable for Carnival, for the ballets alone, which in summer I can have almost at whatever price I wish, in Carnival would cost me personally 700 louis. I am a frank entrepreneur is such cases, and can pay with my own purse, and am not a borrower.

The man of business had returned, replacing the nervy, irritable composer, confident of his ability to make the most beneficial arrangements. Bentivoglio was polite but in no hurry to resume contact with the composer and dissuaded him from attempting to present an opera in the autumn because he would be away. By November, however, he had relented and agreed to act as patron for an opera by Vivaldi in the next Carnival which began 26 December.

Vivaldi threw himself into the preparations for the new opera. As usual, there were problems: this time it was the dancers who were causing trouble. He had engaged the dancer Coluzzi at a fee of 100 louis, with the stipulation that she was to attend all rehearsals as well as performances. Vivaldi was alarmed to hear she had left her family home to make her life with another dancer, Pomeati, whom Vivaldi described as a man 'capable of every mistake and

Santa Maria Formosa, one of Venice's many churches which echoed to splendid music during the great days of the Republic. This church has ancient origins and was rebuilt in 1492 by Mauro Coducci in this form, which would have been familiar to Vivaldi.

every extravagance'. In a letter dated 13 November 1737, Vivaldi assures the nobleman that all will be well on the night, despite the behaviour of the dancer, and the sixteen to eighteen days necessary for the rehearsal of the ballet would be achieved.

Vivaldi was preparing to leave for Ferrara to oversee the preparations for his opera when a bombshell fell on 16 November 1737. He was called before the Papal Nuncio in Venice and told he was forbidden permission to stage the opera in Ferrara by order of the Cardinal Ruffo. At this time Ferrara was part of Papal territory which gave the cardinal the right to behave as he did. Vivaldi wrote in desperation to his patron about the reason for the ban:

...because I am a priest who does not say Mass and because I have the friendship of the singer Girò.

As we know, he explained that ill health was the reason he did not say Mass and had not done so since shortly after becoming ordained.

For this same reason I nearly always live at home, and I only go out in a gondola or coach, because I can no longer walk on account of this chest ailment...No nobleman invites me to his house, not even our prince, because all are informed of my ailment. Immediately after a meal I can usually go out, but never on foot. Such is the reason I never say Mass. I have spent three carnival seasons at Rome for the opera and as Your Eminence knows, I never said Mass...I have been called to Vienna and I never said Mass. I was at Mantua for three years in the service of the exceedingly devout prince of Darmstadt with those same women who have always been treated by His Serene Highness with great benevolence, and I never said Mass.
What troubles me most, is the stain with which His Eminence Cardinal Ruffo marks these poor women: nobody has ever done that. Fourteen years ago we went to a good many European cities, and their modesty was admired everywhere; Ferrara can give sufficient evidence of it. Every day of the week they made their devotions, as sworn and authenticated records can prove.

Apart from the attack on his standing as a priest and the allegations about his friendship with Anna Girò, the ban meant a severe financial blow to Vivaldi, as he explained to Bentivoglio:

I am burdened with the cost of 6,000 ducats in signed engagements for this opera, and at present I have laid out more than 100 sequins. It is impossible to mount the opera without La Girò, since it is impossible to find such another prima donna. It is equally impossible to mount the opera without me, since I do not want to entrust such a large sum to others. Moreover, I am bound by my engagements, from whence springs an ocean of troubles.

Vivaldi urged Bentivoglio to take up his case with Cardinal Ruffo, to persuade him to lift the ban on him or, at least, to ban the opera, which would release Vivaldi from his signed contracts. It seems the cardinal refused to take either action and Bentivoglio suggested another impresario be engaged to mount the opera but Vivaldi could not accept such an idea.

It was a crushing blow but Vivaldi was nothing if not resilient and was already engaged in other musical activities. One of the few foreign journeys undertaken by Vivaldi which is fully authenticated concerns a visit to Amsterdam for the centenary celebrations of the Schouwburg theatre in Amsterdam on 7 January 1738. No doubt the organisers of the celebrations wanted a major figure of European music to attend and it is significant that Vivaldi was selected for the honour. He was, of course, popular in Holland and had a long association with it through the printing house of Le Cène. It was a reversal of fortunes to be fêted as the principal guest at the celebrations, after the ignominy of Ferrara. Vivaldi conducted the orchestra and played a violin concerto composed for the occasion, the splendid D major RV562a, an appropriately theatrical work.

While there is documentary evidence for Vivaldi's visit to Amsterdam, nothing is known about any countries he may have visited on his journey to and from Holland.

After the debacle of Ferrara, he returned to the Venetian opera world, to the theatre where he had enjoyed so many triumphs, S. Angelo. In 1738 he provided three operas – a new opera, *L'oracolo in Messenia*; a revised opera, *Armida al campo d'Egitto* and the pasticcio *Rosmira*. Anna Girò sang in all three of them.

The intervention and prohibition by Cardinal Ruffo must have been shattering. Vivaldi was then sixty, a man who had been spectacularly successful in secular and sacred music. He was, in every sense, a man of the world. He was also a priest and Cardinal Ruffo's ban was a sharp reminder of the vulnerability of his position. The cardinal was known to be a strict cleric in an age when priesthood did not necessarily mean a lifetime of austerity. Vivaldi was the kind of priest he would have liked to discipline: a man who was a priest but who never said Mass; a man who lived with an opera singer in the notoriously lax city of Venice and travelled with her throughout Europe, and was a major influence in the infamous world of opera.

Apart from professional and personal damage caused by the incident, there was the very real question of financial responsibility.

Vivaldi talks of being burdened with contracts of 6,000 ducats for
the proposed opera. It is not known if the contracts were insisted
upon but clearly he feared they would be. If they were, he needed
to be involved in successful productions once more. Even if his
musical powers were waning or his enthusiasm for opera
declining – although there is no evidence of either – he would have
been forced to continue.

The chances of providing opera for Ferrara returned in June
1738, when Cardinal Ruffo resigned his see. Vivaldi immediately
went into action and was soon engaged in arrangements for staging
his opera *Siroe, re di Persia* first performed in 1727, at the Teatro
Pubblico, in Reggio. After the affair of Cardinal Ruffo, Vivaldi
felt it was perhaps not politic to take up too prominent a position
in Ferrara so the production was in the hands of an old associate,
Antonio Mauri. The opera was duly performed in 1739 but Vivaldi

was doomed to failure in Ferrara. The opera was far from successful, so much so that the management were refusing to fulfil the agreed contract of following it with a re-working of *Farnace*.

Writing to Bentivoglio, Vivaldi is astonished that his recitatives should have been so bad, but he finds a culprit for this failure in the performance of the first harpsichordist, Pietro Antonio Berretta, *maestro di cappella* at Ferrara cathedral, who found the recitatives too difficult, according to Vivaldi, tampered with them and made a disaster of recitatives which had been successful at Ancona in 1738. The real fault, though, Vivaldi believes, was in allowing his work to be under the control of another impresario. If he had been present, there would have been no tampering with the recitatives and the music would have been as intended. But now, he declares, his career is in ruins: '*Contutto che al mio nome, et all mia riputaxione mi sta avanti un'Europa, ad ogni modo doppo 94 opere da me composte, non posso soffrire inconveniente simile*' (In all that my name and that my reputation had gone before me through all Europe, and after all the 94 works I have composed it is not possible for me to suffer such a drawback).

The reference to 94 works (which, in the context, must mean opera) is of enormous interest to us as it suggests almost twice the number of operas now documented. If it were simply a piece of exaggeration, Vivaldi would probably have referred to a round figure such as 100, but to use the precise number of 94 indicates that he means the figure he used. It may be that the higher figure includes re-worked operas but, even if that is so, there is the exciting possibility that a body of Vivaldi's operatic work has yet to be discovered.

Vivaldi's fortunes after the disaster of *Siroe* were at a low point, as is shown in this extract from a letter to Bentivoglio dated 2 January 1739:

Excellency, I am at the point of desperation. Nor can I endure such an ignorant person to establish his fortune on the destruction of my poor name. I beg you, for mercy's sake, not to abandon me, for I swear to Your Excellency that if I remain unprotected, I will do extreme things to cover my honour, because whoever takes away my honour may take away my life.

It is a curious passage, almost threatening in tone and there is a desperate sound about the 'extreme things' he threatens to do to protect his honour. The Marchese was not moved to help, however, and warned the composer he should not build his hopes on any further assistance.

Venice remained faithful. *Feraspe*, probably the final opera by Vivaldi, was performed at the S. Angelo theatre in the autumn of 1739 but we do not know how it was received.

His old critic, Benedetto Marcello, died in July 1739 at Brescia. He was only fifty-two and his death might have been gloomy evidence for Vivaldi of the inexorable passing of time.

Vivaldi's popularity was no longer what it was, even in Venice. Proof of this changing state of affairs is found in the account of Charles de Brosses who visited Venice in 1739 and wrote on 29 August:

Vivaldi has become one of my intimate friends in order to sell me some concertos at a very high price. He has in part succeeded, and I too in that which I desired; which was to hear him play and have good musical recreation frequently. He is an old man with a prodigious fury for composition. I have heard him boast of composing a concerto in all its parts more quickly than a copyist could write them down. I found to my great astonishment that he was not as esteemed as he deserves in this country where all is fashion, where his works have been heard for a long time and the music of the preceding years no longer brings in receipts.

Despite the fickle nature of the Venetian public, Vivaldi had been a vastly successful composer, virtuoso and impresario for many years, ever since his first opera was presented in 1726. The public had clamoured, and he had provided, but it now appeared that even he, with all his energy and ability, could no longer please them.

Music was a Venetian obsession. Grand concerts, such as this one painted by Guardi, were given for visiting dignitaries and the ospedali competed to put on the most brilliant programmes.

Chapter 9

Final Departure

The Pietà, which was still one of the musical wonders of Venice, remained. Ferdinand of Bavaria was in the city for the Carnival of 1739 and heard at the Pietà a cantata by Vivaldi, *Il Mopso*, which was greatly admired. The work was described as an *egloga pescatoria* (Fisherman's Idyll), a suitable theme for the city of the sea.

Frederick Christian, son of the King of Poland and Elector of Saxony, arrived in Venice on 19 December 1739. It was a grand and noble visit, the kind of occasion Venice loved. A rich programme of entertainment was provided which included bullfights and jousting and, of course, music. The famous Ospedali were visited, including the Pietà. On 21 March 1740, he visited the Ospedale della Pietà for a concert of music by the famous *Il Prete Rosso* and performed by the *coro di figli* of the charitable institution.

The girls performed a cantata, *Il coro delle muse;* a sinfonia and three concertos.

The dedication of the works, which are in the Dresden National Library, reads:

Concertos with many instruments played by girls of the merciful Ospedale della Pietà in the presence of His Royal Highness the most serene Friedrich Christian, the Royal Prince of Poland and Elector of Saxony. Music by D. Antonio Vivaldi, maestro de' concerti at the above-mentioned hospital. 1740.

The concertos displayed all Vivaldi's qualities; energy, drive, imaginative combinations of instruments. One was written for two violins, two recorders, two trumpets, two mandolins, two salmoè, two theorbos and cello, in addition to string orchestra and basso continuo.

The records of the Pietà confirm that the uneasy relationship Vivaldi had with the institution continued. In 1735 he was narrowly

A glittering concert was performed before Prince Frederick Christian, son of the King of Poland and Elector of Saxony, at the Pietà in 1740. Vivaldi was then 62 and did not have long to live. His popularity in Venice was waning but the concert was a great success and included the brilliant concerto RV558 for violins, recorders, trumpets, mandolines, salmoes, theorboes and cello.

CONCERTI
con molti Istromenti
Suonati dalle Figlie del Pio Ospitale della Pietà
avanti
SUA ALTEZZA REALE
Il Serenißimo
FEDERICO CHRISTIANO
Prencipe Reale di Polonia, et Elettorale di Saßonia.

MUSICA
di D. Antonio Vivaldi
Maestro de Concerti dell'Ospitale sudetto.
In Venezia nell' Anno 1740

elected *maestro de' concerti* but the necessary majority in favour of his appointment was not obtained in 1738 and it may be he was not appointed again; there is no record of any appointment for him at the Pietà in 1739 and 1740. It may be he provided music on request, as in the case of the concert for the prince of Poland, for which a payment of 15 ducats and 13 lire is shown in the accounts for 27 April 1740.

Other composers were being asked to provide music for the Pietà. Tartini provided a sonata in 1735 and there is a record of payment to one Alfonso di Frana 'for music from Paris' in 1741.

The invaluable records of the Pietà also provide information of a momentous decision on Vivaldi's part. The account for 29 April 1740 reads:

It has been brought to our attention that our orchestra needs concertos for organ and other instruments to maintain its present reputation. Since it is understood that the Reverend Vivaldi is about to leave this city of Venice and that he possesses an important number of concertos ready made it would be necessary to acquire these. It is understood that the governors of the *coro* will continue to have the responsibility for buying these concertos, when they think fit, at the cost of one ducat each.

The proposal was lost when the vote was taken, but some further action must have been taken because he was paid 70 ducats and 23 lire for 20 concertos on 12 May, and one ducat for each concerto for 'a great number of concertos' on 29 August. The German musicologist Walter Kolneder comments that these were 'mean prices' in view of the terms of the 1723 agreement in which it was agreed Vivaldi would receive one sequin for each concerto. The

109

money paid for these concertos must have been pitifully small to a man who was accustomed to receiving a payment of 100 sequins for an opera and is an indication of Vivaldi's financial circumstances. Clearly, the governors of the Pietà were driving their customary hard bargain and it is equally clear that Vivaldi was not in a stong bargaining position since he was trying to raise funds to finance his departure from Venice.

His departure from the Pietà and the reasons for it are one of the many mysteries of Vivaldi's life. The connection with the Pietà was finally severed in 1740 and Vivaldi's name appears for the last time in the records on 29 August. He made a brief appearance in an announcement in the *Mercure de France* in December 1740 concerning the publication of a set of six cello sonatas by the firm of Le Clerc Cadet, and the rest is silence.

Most experts believe he went to Vienna, probably to attempt

The Departure of the Bucentaur by Guardi—on Ascension Day of each year the Bucentaur, the Doge's gondola, led a procession of craft in a ceremony which represented the marriage between the Republic and the sea.

to find a place at the court of Charles VI who admired his work and who, as we know, had honoured him in 1728. Fate intervened because Charles VI died suddenly on 20 October 1740, at the age of sixty-five.

It was the worst possible time for Vivaldi to seek to establish himself in the city, although there may have been hope of some patronage from the daughter of Charles VI, Maria Theresa, who succeeded her father and whose husband, the Duke of Lorraine and Grand Duke of Tuscany, had been the subject of previous dedications by Vivaldi.

Equally, the composer may have been travelling towards Dresden, where he had powerful friends, or to Bohemia, the home of his former patron, Count Morzin, or he may simply have been ill.

Maria Theresia (1717-80) with her husband, Francis I. Maria succeeded her father, Charles VI, who was a profound admirer of Vivaldi and had honoured him with a knighthood. It may be that Vivaldi's final journey to Vienna was prompted by the hope of further patronage but Charles VI died suddenly in 1740.

All this is conjecture and for many years it seemed that Vivaldi simply disappeared into obscurity. Indeed, it was not until 1938 that Rudolf Gallo established that Vivaldi died at the end of July 1741, not in Venice, as had been supposed, but in Vienna. He unearthed the records of the burial of Vivaldi in the church of St Stephen in Vienna which show, on 28 July 1741:

The Very Reverend Mr Anthony Vivaldi, secular priest, in Satler's house by the Karner gate, in the Hospital Burial Ground, Kleingleuth. (Vienna, Cathedral and Metropolitan Parish of St Stephen).
Vivaldi's funeral train, July 28
The Very Reverend Mr Anthony Vivaldi, secular priest, died, according to the coroner's verdict, of an internal inflammation in Satler's house by the Karner gate, aged 60 years, in a Hospital Burial Ground.

St. Stephen's Cathedral, Vienna. It was to this city that Vivaldi came in 1740, perhaps hoping to restore his fortunes after being rejected in Venice, and where he died in 1741. He was given a pauper's burial in the hospital burial ground according to records of St. Stephen's.

Then follows the melancholy details including the Kleingleuth, which was a small peal of bells, curates, pall, burial site, gravedigger and sexton, sacristan, pallbearers, storm lanterns and choirboys. By the standards of that time, it was a pauper's burial, as was the burial of another genius, Mozart, fifty years later in the same city. Expenses were kept to 19 florins and 45 kreutzers which can be compared with the 100 florins or more which a nobleman's funeral cost. The house where he died no longer exists, nor does the burial ground, for both were removed during the building of the Ringstrasse in 1858.

A passage from the Memoirs of Gradenigo provides a little more information:

The abbate D. Antonio Vivaldi, the incomparable violinist, known as the red-haired priest, highly esteemed for his concertos and other compositions, earned at one time more than 50,000 ducats, but his inordinate extravagance caused him to die poor, in Vienna.

The figure of 50,000 ducats may have been exaggerated or mistaken, as some observers believe. Certainly, Vivaldi had been enormously successful in his lifetime and must have earned a great deal of money and might have been a rich man, but there is nothing to substantiate the charge of extravagance. We know he talked of the cost of maintaining a household capable of taking care of his needs as an invalid, just as we know he was involved in operatic speculations as an impresario which may not have been uniformly successful, particularly in the later part of his life.

We do not know who was present at the simple funeral with its modest peal of bells and six pallbearers and six choirboys. Anna Girò may well have been present; perhaps with her sister, Paolina, since they were part of Vivaldi's entourage.

The question of what brought him to Vienna remains, just as the larger question of what circumstances led him from the glittering years of fame and wealth to an obscure grave in a corner

Vienna, a painting by Vivaldi's distinguished contemporary, Canaletto.

of a foreign city. There is a theatrical quality in his life with its rise to dizzy heights and its final descent; it could provide the subject for an opera, a moral tale illustrating the transient nature of fame. It has, too, an element of mystery about the cause of his downfall: vanity, arrogance, failure to fulfil the obligations of his office as a priest, a forbidden love for Anna Girò.

Venice today, the same labyrinth of narrow streets, canals and bridges that Vivaldi knew.

Chapter 10

Rebirth

If interest in Vivaldi's music was waning towards the end of his life, it ended completely with his death. His disappearance from the public stage was dramatic, especially in Venice where new composers were claiming the attention of the public. The explanation for this decline is not simply the mercurial character of Venetian taste but reflects the way music was regarded. Music was of the moment; it would be heard and forgotten, replaced by new music.

His eclipse was total in his own country but there was some loyalty to his works in other European countries, especially in Germany. Usually, though, when his name was mentioned it was in dismissive or patronising terms and the judgement of his ability was harsh.

Johann Wolfgang von Goethe (1749-1832) who visited Venice in 1786 and fell under its spell. His account of hearing an oratorio at the Mendicanti, one of the four Ospadele of the city, shows that the tradition of these musical establishments continued into the latter half of the 18th century. The oratorio was sung by nuns behind a grating and was, wrote Goethe "very beautiful, the voices magnificent, the performance of great enjoyment."

England had enjoyed his music greatly – *The Cuckoo* concerto was a national favourite – but the musical establishment's assessment of his merits was severe. In 1753 Charles Avison wrote, a little testily:

It may be proper now to mention by way of example on this head the most noted composers who have erred in the extreme of an unnatural modulation, leaving those of still inferior genius to that oblivion to which they are deservedly destined. Of the first and lowest class are Vivaldi, Tessarini, Alberti and Loccatelli *(sic)*, whose compositions being equally defective in various harmony and true invention, are only a fit amusement for children; nor indeed for these, if ever they are intended to be led to a just taste in music.

Vivaldi was defended in the next year by the distinguished Professor of Music at Oxford, William Hayes, who admitted certain faults of composition but added:

...and yet I think Vivaldi has so much greater merit than the rest that he is worthy of some distinction. Admitting therefore the same kind of levity and manner to be in his compositions with those of Tessarini, etc, yet an essential difference must still be allowed between the former and the latter, inasmuch as an original is certainly preferable to a servile, mean copy.

The professor feels that Vivaldi is of a volatile disposition, 'having too much mercury in his constitution' but praises his achievements in solid composition, singling out the eleventh of his first twelve concertos, Opus 3. Of this, he says: 'The principal subjects of which are well invented, well maintained, the whole properly diversified with masterly contrivances, and the harmony full and complete.'

Doctor Burney in his history of music was favourable, but Hawkins, in his history of music (both published in 1776) was not. His disappearance from the attention of scholars was not as complete as the disappearance of performances of his works and it seemed his music was destined for some dusty corner of a library, an arcane subject for a future scholar.

This oblivion lasted for about a hundred years. Musical dictionaries and biographies often failed to mention his name. Leopold Mozart's violin study, published in 1756 (the year his son, Wolfgang Amadeus, was born), contained nothing from Vivaldi but did have examples from his contemporary, Giuseppe Tartini. The emergence of Vivaldi's music, when it eventually came, was accidental and occurred because of a growing appreciation of the genius of the great Johann Sebastian Bach

Leopold Mozart (1719-87), father of Wolfgang, whose treatise on the violin appeared in 1756. It is notable that it contained no reference to Vivaldi, one of the most brilliant virtuosos of the first quarter of the 18th century, although there is a reference to Vivaldi's contemporary, Tartini.

during the 19th century. It was noted that Bach had adapted some of Vivaldi's compositions for his own use, a discovery which drew attention towards the little known Venetian composer.

One of the first scholars to draw attention to Bach's interest in Vivaldi was Johann Nikolaus Forkel, who wrote in 1802 of Bach's early attempts at composition and the difficulties he had encountered. He wrote:

Vivaldi's violin concertos, just then being published, gave him the guidance he needed. He so often heard them cited as outstanding compositions that he thereby hit upon the happy idea of transcribing them as a group for the keyboard. Hence he studied the progression of the ideas and their relations, variety in modulating and many other things.

117

The great Johann Sebastian Bach (1685-1750) who was sufficiently impressed by Vivaldi's l'Estro Armonico that he transcribed some of the works for keyboard. It was his interest in Vivaldi which led to the re-discovery of the Italian composer after many years of neglect.

Forkel was much more generous to Vivaldi than later German scholars, some of whom adopted a patronising attitude towards the Venetian. Julius Ruhlmann in 1867 found Vivaldi's music 'almost entirely dead' and minimised the influence Vivaldi might have had on Bach by placing the transcriptions late in the career of the German.

It has since been established that Bach worked on most of the transcriptions before 1717 when he was a young man at Weimar. Six of these transcriptions are taken from Vivaldi's Opus 3, *L'estro armonico* which was such an outstanding success when it was published in 1710. This success may well have been known to Bach perhaps in manuscript form because it is likely the work was in circulation in this form well before publication. The influence of Northern Italy, especially Venice, on Germany was profound and there was a constant traffic of people and ideas between the two countries. J. J. Quantz, who is one example of this traffic, has described how impressed he was by Vivaldi's concertos in 1714.

The tenth concerto of Opus 3 was identified as the source of Bach's concerto for four harpsichords in 1850. It is rewarding to compare these two works, each of which is individually successful while sharing common features. Opinions on the value of Vivaldi's contributions has been varied, as has opinion of the success of some of Bach's transcriptions. In certain cases, admirers of Bach felt it was necessary to deny Vivaldi's importance since to acknowledge it might detract from the contribution of their idol. The truth is that Vivaldi served as an excellent model which Bach was eager to follow, particularly in studying the solo concerto form which Vivaldi virtually created.

Arnold Schering's study of Vivaldi in 1905 emphasised the Italian composer's range of compositions and drew attention to his development of the violin concerto.

Vivaldi's music began to be published again and a catalogue of works known to have been printed in his lifetime appeared in 1922.

The next chapter in the rehabilitation of Vivaldi is as dramatic as anything in the composer's life. The hero of this story is a professor of music at Turin University, Alberto Gentili, who devoted much of his life, and his considerable powers of detection, to Vivaldi's music.

It was known that a court orchestra in Turin had flourished in the 18th century and that its musical archives had been hidden when the court retreated to Sardinia at the time of the Napoleonic wars. Unfortunately, when the orchestra returned, the place where the music had been hidden could not be traced. There was a tradition it was hidden in a monastery, where it was hidden still, a trail Gentili pursued with diligence and with ultimate success when the head of the Collegio S. Carlo in Monferrato approached the Turin National Library for assistance in valuing a collection of musical manuscripts in the autumn of 1926. The monks needed to sell the collection, which had been presented to them by the family of Marchese Durazzo, to carry out essential repairs to the monastery. The collection came from Conte Giacomo Durazzo (1717-94), an intriguing character who had associations with Venice and Vienna. Through his wife, the Genoese nobleman entered the service of Austria and became director and administrator of the court theatre and court orchestra. He was a man of considerable musical taste, encouraging Gluck and Mozart, and an inveterate collector. When he was appointed Austrian ambassador to Venice in 1765, it is certain he would have known of the musical delights of the Ospedali, including the Pietà.

The collection from the monastery was enormous and its 95 volumes included 14 by Vivaldi. Gentili had to find a private patron to buy the collection since the library did not have sufficient funds for the purpose and found one in Robert Foa who agreed to fund the project as a memorial to his son, Mauro, who had recently died.

Gentili's examination of the volumes revealed a fascinating

119

oddity. The scores, bound in pigskin, were numbered in pairs but some of the numbers lacked their corresponding pair. The conclusion was inescapable; the collection had been divided and there were other manuscripts by Vivaldi in existence which should be restored to the 140 instrumental works, 29 cantatas, 12 operas, one oratorio and other works which had been discovered so far.

Research into the genealogy of the Durazzo family began, to establish if there were any remaining members of the family living who might have part of the musical inheritance in their possession. Such a person was found: Marchese Giuseppe Maria Durazzo, an ancient patrician, the last of the line. Durazzo had inherited a large library from his father which could well contain the complementary Vivaldi compositions but the old man had no intention of allowing anyone to see his collection. He was outraged by the sale of the Monferrato collection, claiming the monks had no right to dispose of them. With the help of the old man's father confessor, the Jesuit priest, Antonio Oldro, pressure was brought to bear and he reluctantly allowed an inspection of the library which did, indeed, contain the expected manuscripts.

Identification of the treasure was only the first part of the battle and three years were to pass before the Marchese agreed to let the collection go on payment of a substantial sum to the Turin National Library. Again, a patron was found: a textiles manufacturer, Filippo Giordano, and arrangements were successfully concluded on 30 April 1930. A tragic coincidence was that Filippo Giordano had also lost a son and the combined collection was entitled 'the Collezione Mauro Foa e Renzo Giordano'.

The old nobleman was difficult to the end, insisting that a condition of the sale was that the works should never be published or performed. What lay behind the old man's passionate attempts to keep the works from public scrutiny is unknown, but the ban was attacked in the courts and eventually lifted.

At last, in September 1939, a festival of Vivaldi's works was held in Siena which was taken from the music in the complete Durazzo collection, including performances of the opera, *L'Olimpiade*.

The war years interrupted the renaissance of Vivaldi's music but it continued after the war. A biography by Mario Rinaldi, *Antonio Vivaldi*, appeared in Milan in 1943, and was followed – or rather, overtaken – in 1948 by the classic study of Marc Pincherle, whose book was the result of forty years of study of the composer. Not surprisingly, the latter is the definitive work and it is a book in which immense scholarship is carried lightly and expressed in elegant style. The Frenchman has done more than anyone to restore Vivaldi to us but there have been others who have helped. The

The Esterhazy Palace at Eisendstadt (a steel engraving by C. Rohrich after L. Rohbock) where Franz Joseph Haydn (1732-1809) was responsible as Kapellmeister for the music. The Esterhazy family were related to Count von Morzin, to whom Vivaldi's The Four Seasons is dedicated.

German, Walter Kolneder, has provided insights into much of Vivaldi's music, especially his operatic music. Michael Talbot in his *Vivaldi*, published in 1978, and Alan Kendall in his *Vivaldi* biography, published in the same year, continued the work.

The enthusiasm for Vivaldi and baroque music shows no sign of diminishing. Indeed, interest in the period is increasing: public demand for this kind of music is shown in the catalogues of the record companies as well as in the programmes of radio stations and the works of large and small orchestras. Order has been brought to the great mass of Vivaldi's work by the Danish musicologist, Peter Ryom, whose cataloguing of them is now widely accepted, although the great Pincherle's numbering is still used occasionally. Discoveries are made regularly. Twelve violin sonatas and two violin concertos came to light in 1973 and a sonata for violin, oboe and organ was discovered in 1976.

In his lifetime Vivaldi's reputation rested on his skill as a violinist, but there was a powerful demand for his compositions of secular and sacred music as his efforts on behalf of the Pietà and the theatres of Venice amply illustrate.

Vivaldi is best known as a composer of concertos, more than 450 of them, especially for his development of the solo concerto. Not surprisingly, most have the violin as the solo instrument but the cello, viola d'amore, mandolin, flautino, recorder, flute, oboe and bassoon were all given solo status. There were also concertos for two solo instruments and for three or more. The principal characteristic of the Vivaldian type of solo concerto is its emphasis on the freedom of the individual instrument, a freedom which clearly appealed to Vivaldi the virtuoso, enabling him to display the full range of his talent.

The concerto of the period is in three movements: allegro, andante, allegro. The apparent rigidity of the form, and Vivaldi's compositions in it, has led to a hostile reception in some quarters.

Describing what he considered to be the decline of music in Italy, J. J. Quantz, writing in 1752, does not mention Vivaldi (whom he had formerly admired) or Tartini by name but it can only be these two violinists he is writing about:

Two celebrated Lombardic violinists who began to be known about thirty or forty years ago, one not long after the other, have independently contributed much to this state of affairs. The first was lively and rich in invention and supplied almost half the world with his concertos. Although Torelli, and after him Corelli, has made a start in this genre of music, this violinist, together with Albinoni, has made it a better form and produced good models in it. And in this way he also achieved general credit, just as Corelli had with his twelve solos. But finally, as a result of excessive daily composing, and especially after he had begun to write theatrical vocal pieces, he sank into frivolity and eccentricity both in composition and performances and in consequence his last concertos did not gain as much approbation as the first. Whatever the case may be, because of his character this change in his manner of thinking in his last years almost completely deprived the above-mentioned celebrated violinist of good taste in both performance and composition.

Vivaldi's spate of compositions has raised doubts in many minds. Luigi Dallapiccola (1904-75) is given credit for the remark that Vivaldi was the 'composer not of six hundred concertos but of one concerto written six hundred times'. The witticism is not original but the opinion is shared by Igor Stravinsky (1882-1971) who, in Robert Craft's *Conversations with Stravinsky*, described Vivaldi as 'greatly over-rated – a dull fellow who could compose the same form so many times over'.

What these distinguished musicians appear to have missed is Vivaldi's extraordinary inventiveness within an established form. In a body of work as large as that of Vivaldi and in the conditions in which the work was composed, there is likely to be some

A view of Venice, from the Zattere towards the Doge's Palace, by Turner.

Venice has exerted its charms on many composers since Vivaldi. Wagner and Verdi are honoured by statues in the public gardens, laid out by order of Napoleon, which lie beyond the Riva degli Schiavoni to the east. Wagner composed part of *Tristan* in the city, and Verdi's *La Traviata* was first performed at the Fenice theatre in the city.

variation of quality but few composers have maintained the highest possible level in all their work except, perhaps, Mozart. Closer study of Vivaldi's compositions, especially for the solo concerto, lead to an overwhelming admiration at the level of melody, rhythm and harmonic writing maintained.

The critics also betray an unfamiliarity with the historical context of the works which brings a magisterial rebuke from Walter Kolneder on Stravinsky, whose views, he says '...can only be attributed to a complete ignorance of the circumstances of a creator in the eighteenth century' and he adds that composers who worked quickly, such as Vivaldi, Scarlatti, Bach, Haydn and Mozart, did so because they were obliged to do so to make a living.

In freeing himself from the polyphonic style, Vivaldi created a personal style of great individuality. His music is immediately recognisable; the voice as distinctive as that of Mozart or Beethoven. A distinguishing element of this style is the highly charged, intense rhythmic drive. This rhythm is described by J. J. Quantz who says:

...he was one of those who invented the Lombard style, which consists of the following: where there are two or three notes one occasionally shortens the note that comes on the beat and puts a dot after the note that comes between the beats. This style began about the year 1722. But it seems to resemble Scottish music somewhat as certain features of this style reveal.

Pincherle points to Vivaldi's variations of this rhythmic style in a concerto at Turin where the composer has added the instruction 'Pay attention to the slur' *(guardata la legature)* on the score. Pincherle is also responsible for the phrase 'rhythmic ardour' as a description of Vivaldi's violin music, a perfect description of Vivaldi's particular style.

Vivaldi's habit of composing for different instruments and for different groups was probably a matter of necessity, dictated by the availability of players of special ability and by the musical means at his disposal at the Pietà or the theatre.

He wrote a great deal for the cello, elevating the instrument from its former position as a humble accompanist and giving it the solo position. He virtually created the cello concerto and was probably inspired by the compositions of Giuseppe Jacchini (died 1727) who was a virtuoso cellist and composer for the instrument. None of Vivaldi's cello compositions, concertos or sonatas were published in his lifetime. It is likely they were written for gifted pupils at the Pietà and for Antonio Vandini, a cellist who was employed at the Pietà as a teacher in 1720-22. It is possible Vivaldi played

The four horses of St. Mark's by Canaletto positioned on individual plinths as they were in Vivaldi's lifetime. They are now mounted on a balcony in the façade of St. Mark's.

Venice: A storm approaching San Giorgio and the Dogana by Turner.

the cello: there is also evidence that he played the harpsichord from a reference to him accompanying Anna Girò from the keyboard at a recital.

The cello works are typically Vivaldian, blending brilliant, attacking rhythm and languorous adagios. The G minor for two cellos is a dazzling example of his work for the instrument.

Another instrument which benefited from the maestro's attention was the viola d'amore, an instrument which is little heard today; a pity, because its silvery tone is peculiarly appealing. The individual tone of the instrument is produced by a set of strings below the playing strings, which vibrate when the instrument is played. Stringed instruments feature in the majority of his compositions but Vivaldi also composed prodigiously for recorder and flute, oboe, clarinet and bassoon.

Scholars see Vivaldi as significant in the development of the classical symphony; Charles de Brosses in 1739 refers to the Pietà as 'the first as regards the perfecting of symphonies'.

126

His influence in the development of descriptive or programme music is easily observed in the works of composers such as Haydn and Beethoven. There is something of an apologetic tone in discussions about programme music today as if it is somehow less worthy than abstract or 'pure' music. In *The Four Seasons* Vivaldi was concerned to depict the seasons as accurately as possible and does so with extraordinary skill and ingenuity. At the same time, the music does more than express the physical world: the buzzing of flies, the barking of dogs. It expresses the spirit of the seasons, the lassitude of heavy summer; the nervy, trembling arrival of spring.

It was not until the dramatic discoveries of Alberto Gentili in Turin in the 1920s that Vivaldi's significance as a composer of vocal music was appreciated. His compositions in this area were on the usual scale: 48 operas, 39 cantatas, more than 60 sacred works. As is often the case with Vivaldi, contemporary opinion was not always completely favourable. We have heard Quantz's view that Vivaldi's operatic interests led to a falling off in his concertos and Vivaldi's fellow violinist and composer, Tartini, is not an admirer of his vocal music. 'I have been urged to work for the Venetian theatres,' he told Charles de Brosses, 'and I have never been willing to do it, well knowing that a gullet is not the neck of a violin. Vivaldi, who wanted to practise in both areas, always failed in one, whereas in the other he succeeded very well.'

Vivaldi's record as a leading composer of operas for some twenty-five years hardly supports the charge of failure. The sacred music which he composed for the Pietà during his long association with that establishment exhibits the familiar elements of Vivaldi's style: richness of harmony, dramatic presentation, vigour and melodic invention.

Vivaldi's place in musical history is now established. His influence is recognised in a long line of composers from Haydn and Beethoven to Sir Michael Tippet whose 2nd Symphony with its 'pounding Cs' is a tribute to Vivaldi who showed a strong partiality for the key of C. Perhaps more important is that his music has not lost its common touch and is as popular with listeners today as it was when the Venetians clamoured for more in the 18th century.

The Venice of his time has gone; banished with the arrival of Napoleon I, who looked at the city and said: 'I want no more inquisitors, no more Senate: I will be an Attila for the Venetian state.' His troops entered Venice in 1797 and met no opposition, the first time the city had been occupied in its long history.

Robert Browning, who loved the city, provided a perfect epitaph for Venice from the vantage point of the 19th century in his much-quoted poem, 'A Toccata of Galuppi's'; the toccata referred to

Napoleon Bonaparte (1769-1821), detail from a portrait by Anne Louis Girodet-Troison. Through all the centuries of the Republic, Venice had never been occupied by enemy troops but that record ended with the arrival of the French army in May, 1797 fulfilling Napoleon's grim prophecy: "I want no more Inquisitors, no more Senate: I will be an Attila for the Venetian State."

is imaginary but Galuppi, one of Vivaldi's successors, is not.

'Dust and ashes, dead and done with, Venice spent what Venice earned.
The soul, doubtless, is immortal – where a soul can be discerned.'
As for Venice and her people, merely born to bloom and drop,
Here on earth they bore their fruitage, mirth and folly were the crop:
What of soul was left, I wonder when the kissing had to stop?

Venice and Vivaldi, the two words are closely linked in the mind but Venice is a curiosity, magical but ghostly, a jewelled and fantastic relic, while Vivaldi's music is vibrant, surging with life and energy, as passionate and compelling as when it first echoed in the city of the sea.

His personal story is remarkable, full of mystery and drama, and has a particular fascination because it is likely to go on. It is quite possible that more works by Vivaldi will be discovered, perhaps the missing operas, and answers provided for some of the many puzzles that occur in the story of *Il Prete Rosso*.

Vivaldi works

The RV numbers used in this list of works by Vivaldi are those of the Danish musicologist, P. Ryom, who has organised a comprehensive listing of the composer's works which supersedes previous catalogues.

INSTRUMENTAL MUSIC

Sonatas for violin

RV No	Key				
1	C	16	e	30	A
2	C	17	e	31	A
3	C	17a	e	32	a
4	C	18	F	33	B
5	c	19	F	34	B
6	c	20	F	35	b
7	c	21	f	36	b
8	c	22	G	37	b
9	D	23	G	754	C
10	D	24	G	755	D
11	D	25	G	756	E
12	d	26	g	757	g
13	d	27	g	758	A
14	d	28	g	759	B
15	d	29	g	760	b

Sonatas for cello

38	d	43	a
39	e	44	a
40	e	45	b
41	F	46	b
42	g	47	b

129

Sonatas for one instrument

48	C	54	C	
49	d	55	C	
50	e	56	C	
51	g	57	G	
52	F	58	g	
53	c	59	A	

Sonatas for two violins

60	C	70	F	
61	C	71	G	
62	D	72	g	
63	d	73	g	
64	d	74	g	
65	E	75	A	
66	E	76	B	
67	e	77	B	
68	F	78	B	
69	F	79	b	

Sonatas for two instruments

80	G
81	g
82	C
83	c
84	D
85	g
86	a

Sonatas for more than two instruments

130	E
169	b

Concertos without orchestra

87	C	91	D	95	D
88	C	92	D	96	d
89	D	93	D	97	F
90	D	94	D	98	F

130

99	F	104	g
100	F	105	g
101	G	106	g
102	G	107	g
103	g	108	g

Concertos and sinfonias for string orchestra

109	C	128	d	149	G
110	C	129	d	150	G
111	C	131	E	151	G
111a	C	132	E	152	g
112	C	133	e	153	g
113	C	134	e	154	g
114	C	135	F	155	g
115	C	136	F	156	g
116	C	137	F	157	g
117	C	138	F	158	A
118	c	139	F	159	A
119	c	140	F	160	A
120	c	141	F	161	a
121	D	142	F	162	B
122	D	143	f	163	B
123	D	144	G	164	B
124	D	145	G	165	B
125	D	146	G	166	B
126	D	147	G	167	B
127	d	148	G	168	b

The Rialto Bridge by Guardi, a scene which must have been familiar to Vivaldi.

Concertos for violin and string orchestra

170	C	186	C	761	c
171	C	187	C	203	D
172	C	188	C	204	D
172a	C	189	C	205	D
173	C	190	C	206	D
174	C	191	C	207	D
175	C	192	C	208	D
176	C	193	C	208a	D
177	C	194	C	209	D
178	C	195	C	210	D
179	C	196	c	211	D
180	C	197	c	212	D
181	C	198	c	212a	D
181a	C	198a	c	213	D
182	C	199	c	214	D
183	C	200	c	215	D
184	C	201	c	216	D
185	C	202	c	217	D

This view of the interior of the theatre of Verona shows a typically luxurious interior with galleried seats in several tiers, similar in style to La Fenice in Venice.

218	D	269	E	318	g
219	D	270	E	319	g
220	D	271	E	320	g
221	D	762	E	321	g
222	D	273	e	322	g
223	D	274	e	323	g
224	D	275	e	324	g
224a	D	275a	e	325	g
225	D	276	e	326	g
226	D	277	e	327	g
227	D	278	e	328	g
228	D	279	e	329	g
229	D	280	e	330	g
230	D	281	e	331	g
231	D	282	F	332	g
232	D	283	F	333	g
233	D	284	F	334	g
234	D	285	F	335	A
752	D	285a	F	336	A
235	d	286	F	337	A
236	d	287	F	339	A
237	d	288	F	340	A
238	d	289	F	341	A
239	d	290	F	342	A
240	d	291	F	343	A
241	d	292	F	344	A
242	d	293	F	345	A
243	d	294	F	346	A
244	d	294a	F	347	A
245	d	295	F	348	A
246	d	296	F	349	A
247	d	297	f	350	A
248	d	298	G	351	A
249	d	299	G	352	A
250	E	300	G	353	A
251	E	301	G	763	A
252	E	302	G	768	A
253	E	303	G	354	a
254	E	304	G	355	a
255	E	305	G	356	a
256	E	306	G	357	a
257	E	307	G	358	a
258	E	308	G	359	B
259	E	309	G	360	B
260	E	310	G	361	B
261	E	311	G	362	B
262	E	312	G	363	B
263	E	313	G	364	B
263a	E	314	G	364a	B
264	E	314a	G	365	B
265	E	315	g	366	B
266	E	316	g	367	B
267	E	316a	g	368	B
268	E	317	g	369	B

370	B		382	B	
371	B		383	B	
372	B		383a	B	
373	B		384	b	
374	B		385	b	
375	B		386	b	
376	B		387	b	
377	B		388	b	
378	B		389	b	
379	B		390	b	
380	B		391	b	
381	B				

Concertos for viola d'amore and string orchestra

392	D
393	d
394	d
395	d
395a	d
396	A
397	a

Concertos for cello and string orchestra

398	C	407	d	416	g
399	C	408	E	417	g
400	C	409	e	418	a
401	c	410	F	419	a
402	c	411	F	420	a
403	D	412	F	421	a
404	D	413	G	422	a
405	d	414	G	423	B
406	d	415	G	242	b

Concerto for mandolin and string orchestra

425	C

Concertos for flute and string orchestra

426	D	434	F
427	D	435	G
428	D	436	G
429	D	437	G
430	e	438	G
431	e	439	g
432	e	440	a
433	F		

Concertos for recorder and string orchestra

441	c
442	F

Concertos for 'flautino' and string orchestra

443	C
444	C
445	a

Concertos for oboe and string orchestra

446	C	456	F
447	C	457	F
448	C	458	F
449	C	459	g
450	C	460	g
451	C	461	a
452	C	462	a
453	D	463	a
454	d	464	B
455	F	465	B

Concertos for bassoon and string orchestra

466	C	471	C	476	C
467	C	472	C	477	C
468	C	473	C	478	C
469	C	474	C	479	C
470	C	475	C	480	c

135

481	d	489	F	497	a
482	d	490	F	498	a
483	E	491	F	499	a
484	e	492	G	500	a
485	F	493	G	501	B
486	F	494	G	502	B
487	F	495	g	503	B
488	F	496	g	504	B

Concertos for two violins and string orchestra

505	C	514	d	523	a
506	C	515	E♭	524	B♭
507	C	516	G	525	B♭
508	C	517	g	526	B♭
509	c	518	A	527	B♭
510	c	519	A	528	B♭
511	D	520	A	529	B♭
512	D	521	A	530	B♭
513	D	522	a	764	B♭

Other concertos for two instruments and string orchestra

531	g	538	F	544	F
532	G	539	F	767	F
533	C	766	c	545	G
534	C	540	d	546	A
535	d	541	d	547	B
536	a	542	F	548	B
537	C	543	F		

Concertos for several violins and string orchestra

549	D
550	e
551	F
552	A
553	B

Other concertos for several instruments and string orchestra

554	C	556	C	559	C
554a	C	557	C	560	C
555	C	558	C	561	C

562	D		567	F		574	F
562a	D		568	F		575	G
563	D		569	F		576	g
564	D		570	F		577	g
564a	D		571	F		578	g
565	d		572	F		579	B
566	• d		573	F		580	b

Concertos for violin and two string orchestras

581	C
582	D
583	B

S. Giovanni di Bragora, a painting by Pierre Besrodny. It was at this church in a quiet square, not far from the Riva degli Schiavoni, that Vivaldi's certificate of baptism was discovered in the 1960s, showing he was born in 1678.

Concertos for several instruments and two orchestras

584	F
585	A

SACRED VOCAL WORKS

586	C	607	F	627	G
587	g	608	g	628	G
588	D	609	e	629	g
589	D	610	g	630	E
590	—	610a	g	631	E
591	e	610b	g	632	F
592	G	611	g	633	F
593	G	612	C	634	A
594	D	613	B	635	A
595	D	614	F	636	G
596	C	615	C	637	B
597	C	616	c	638	c
598	B	617	F	639	D
599	B	618	g	639a	D
600	c	619	?	640	g
601	G	620	C	641	F
602	A	621	f	642	D
602a	A	622	?	646	—
603	A	623	A	647	—
604	C	624	e	648	—
605	C	625	F		
606	d	626	c		

SECULAR VOCAL WORKS

643	663	679
644	664	680
645	665	681
649	666	682
650	667	683
651	668	684
652	669	685
653	753	686
654	670	687
655	671	688
656	672	689
657	673	690
658	674	691
659	675	692
660	676	693
661	677	694
662	678	

OPERAS

RV No	Title		
729	Ottone in Villa	711	Farnace
727	Orlando finto pazzo	709	Dorilla in Tempe
724	Nerone fatto Cesare	722	Ipermestra
706	La costanza trionfante degl'amori e degl'odi	735	Siroe, re di Persia
		728	Orlando furioso
700	Arsilda	730	Rosilena en Oronta
719	L'incoronazione di Dario	702	Atenaide
737	Tieteberga	733	Semiramide
701	Artabana Re de Parti	714	La fida ninfa
732	Scanderbeg	696	Alvida
699	Armida al Campo d'Egitto	697	Argippo
706	La Candace o siano Li veri amici	708	Doriclea
		723	Montezuma
739	La verita in cimento	725	L'Olimpiade
720	Gli inganni per vendetta	718	Griselda
715	Filippo, Re di Macedonia	703	Tamerlano (Bajazet)
734	Silvia	695	Adelaide
710	Ercole sul Termodonte	698	Aristide
718	Giustino	716	Ginevra, principessa di Scozia
740	La virtù trionfante dell'amore e dell'odio, ovvero Il Tigrane	705	Catone in Utica
		731	Rosmira
721	L'inganno trionfante in amore	726	L'oracolo in Messenia
		713	Feraspe
707	Cunegonda	736	Teuzzone
712	La fede tradita e vendicata	738	Tito Manlio

Walter Kolneder, in his book, published in Germany in 1965 and by Faber and Faber in English in 1970, lists the following as operas by Vivaldi

Vinto trionfante del Vincitore
L'odio vinto della costanza
Sarce
Demetrio
Alessandro nell' Indie

140

Index

One of the most magnificent sights in Venice, Santa Maria della Salute, built to celebrate the end of a plague that had swept away 47,000 citizens, between 1631 and 1681.